building a
healthy
lawn

a safe and natural approach

BY STUART FRANKLIN

STOREY BOOKS

The mission of Storey Publishing is to serve our customers by publishing practical information that encourages personal independence in harmony with the environment.

Acknowledgments

Special thanks to Eliot Roberts, Director of The Lawn Institute, for his immediate offer of technical help and guidance; to Deborah Burns and Jeff Silva, my editors and friends at Garden Way; to J. I. Rodale, pioneer of the "organic" movement; to L. Ron Hubbard, whose Study Technology made all my research much easier.

My appreciation to C. R. Funk of Rutgers University, H. Tashiro of Cornell University, Dave David, Ben Carter, John Beume, Jeanine Zoda, Farmer Beiling, Lewis Crowell, Jeff Frank, Green Pro Services, John Jones, and Mark Miles.

Cover design by Deborah Haskel
Text design by Wanda Harper
Front and back cover photos by Jerry Howard, Positive Images
Illustrations by Alison Kolesar
Edited by Deborah Burns and Jeff Silva
Typesetting by Jackson Typesetting Co.

Copyright © 1988 by Storey Publishing, LLC

Second Edition

Printed in the United States by Versa Press, Inc.
20 19 18 17 16 15 14

Library of Congress Cataloging-in-Publication Data

Franklin, Stuart, 1951–
  Building a healthy lawn.

"A Garden Way Publishing book."
Bibliography: p.
Includes index.
  1. Lawns 2. Organic gardening. I. Title
SB433.F73 1988   635.9'647   87-46446
ISBN 0-88266-518-9

About the Author

Stuart Franklin has been an advocate of natural lawn care and gardening practices for the past twenty years. He owns and operates a lawn fertilizing company in western New York. His hands-on experience with hundreds of homeowner lawns has helped him separate theory from workability, resulting in the methods described in this book. Stuart graduated from Syracuse University in 1973. He lives in Williamsville, New York with his wife Jean and three children, Adam, Aaron, and Madeline.

To my wife Jean, for all the extra work you did willingly so I would have the time to write this book.

TABLE OF CONTENTS

FOREWORD

Have you ever listened to your lawn? The sounds of crickets and frogs in wetlands call our attention to the ecology of these places. Lawns, however, are rather quiet places, and we don't normally think of them as places populated with plant and animal life, teeming with activity.

A lawn cut at a two-inch height is actually a very small forest; within its vegetative canopy are fascinating organisms that influence each other's lives and respond dramatically to changes in the environment. These organisms help to maintain a dynamic, living soil that is favorable to the growth of your lawn. They probably don't do this on purpose, and they don't send a bill at the end of the month for services rendered, but they are there, slowly releasing nutrients for lawngrasses, biodegrading a wide variety of pollutants and pesticides, and decomposing organic matter to form humus.

In a good healthy lawn there are well over 900 billion of these organisms for each pound of soil. Most of them are too small to see without the aid of a powerful microscope, but we know they're there because we can measure the benefits they create in helping to build a healthy lawn.

Building a healthy lawn depends on the presence and activity of these billions of tiny plants and animals that are part of a lawn's ecology. We should water the lawn carefully—not too little, not too much. The same is true for fertilizing. Slowly available nutrients from lawn fertilizers formulated with natural organic materials, or slow-release synthetic products, are best for lawns.

When it comes to pest control, first let the harmful pathogens or insects compete with other organisms without your intervention. Wherever balances favor beneficial life forms, pesticides will not be needed. At times, balances will end up favoring harmful pathogens and insects, and then pesticides may need to be considered.

The best weed control is the practice of maintaining healthy turf. Grow a grass plant and no weed can establish itself at that point.

There may be one weed seed ready to germinate for each square inch of your soil throughout the entire growing season—the potential for weed infestation in lawns is overwhelming. By growing grass plants, this potential for weed development is greatly reduced, and herbicides will seldom be necessary.

You are one of more than fifty-six million Americans with a home lawn. This book will help you to understand how to build a healthy lawn that will bring personal satisfaction and enhance your quality of life.

Eliot C. Roberts, Ph.D.
Executive Director
The Lawn Institute
Pleasant Hill, Tennessee

The Lawn Institute was formed in 1955 as a non-profit corporation to assist in and encourage, through research and public education, the improvement of lawns and sports turf. This has been accomplished by providing information on grasses, chemical products, equipment, and techniques for planting and maintaining lawns and turf. Such information has been prepared especially for garden writers, broadcasters, consultants, classroom instructors, Cooperative Extension specialists and agents, and the general public through individual or group contact.

INTRODUCTION

Lawn care is a confusing task for most homeowners. They mow their lawns, but aren't sure when mowing should be done, or how high to cut. They water, but without certainty about how much to water or how often to do it. When it comes to fertilizing or controlling weeds and insects, they place their faith in the most highly advertised products, or simply pay to have a chemical spraying company come four or five times a season—and then worry about any harmful effects the chemicals might have. Sometimes the sprayed lawn ends up with new problems, frustrating the homeowners who thought they were paying to get rid of their lawn problems. Lacking basic knowledge about how lawns grow, people rely on the "experts," or on their neighbors, or they just hope for the best. To add to the confusion, there are those who know nothing about the subject yet have beautiful lawns. Is it all just luck, or is there something else involved?

Previous books on lawn care have paralleled the advice of the chemically oriented lawn industry. These books emphasize locating and diagnosing a lawn's problem, and selecting the proper chemical to kill it off. This is a negative approach that leads us to believe that we have little control over which problem will befall our lawn next. We are supposed to wait for a problem to occur, and then treat it with a chemical.

This book presents a more positive approach to lawn care. You'll be taught how to *keep* your lawn healthy, and you'll learn how most lawn problems are preventable and curable without the use of chemicals. This is a very workable, safe, and sane approach to lawn care.

When a spraying service kills off pests or disease in a lawn, they don't stop to ask why these unwanted elements exist to begin with. They don't see that what they are treating—weeds, insects, and disease—are just symptoms of a weak, unhealthy lawn and soil. Most lawn care books give very little importance to this basic truth:

A healthy lawn will crowd out most weeds and resist insects and disease.

1

The way to simplify lawn care is to get a good grasp on what a healthy lawn is and how to keep it that way. This approach is very similar to the way you care for your own body. Learn how to keep it healthy, and you'll rarely be sick. Body health comes through exercise, proper nutrition, and so on. Chemicals (medicines) are rarely needed to keep a person healthy; they are used to get rid of sickness once it occurs. In fact, if you were to take medicines such as penicillin regularly, as a preventive measure, your body's own defenses would probably deteriorate, resulting in diminished health. This is what happens to many of today's chemically treated lawns. Because people know less about lawns, however, than they do about the human body, they unwittingly ruin, or allow the deterioration of, their lawns.

The true nature of a healthy lawn has not been broadly promoted by the lawn care industry. You are usually told that your lawn should be lush and green in all seasons, and that anything that might cause the lawn harm should be stamped out immediately. The poor home-owner worries about weeds, insects, fungus, and disease, and spends many useless hours trying to combat them. I say useless because these problems are, after all, just symptoms. Symptoms will reoccur until the real causes are corrected. You can stop being a slave to your lawn and its various ills simply by working to create a healthy lawn. This means giving it the proper environment and care for good growth. Chemicals have very little to do with lawn health, except in emergency situations when there is no natural solution available. By concentrating on keeping your lawn healthy, you make lawn care much easier. Many common lawn problems will never attack a healthy lawn. In fact, most of these so-called problems are due to lack of gardening knowledge.

This book is meant to supply enough basic lawn care information to enable you to think for yourself on the subject. And part of that knowledge will include knowing when it is time to call in a "lawn doctor" to help diagnose problems and possibly treat your lawn. Even lawn doctors are sometimes uncertain about what to do, but that is no cause for alarm. There is no magic formula that tells how to care for a lawn. We are dealing with a living thing that we want to flourish under many different conditions. If you know your basics, you'll be able to handle your lawn's particular needs as they come up. You'll know when to cut and water. You'll know how high to cut and how much to water. You'll know why one neighbor who applies chemicals has a disease-ridden lawn, while another one who doesn't bother with chemicals has a lovely lawn. Using all this simple information, you will continue to improve your lawn and maintain it easily as the years go by.

The idea of creating health to prevent illness is not new. In the field of lawn care, however, it is just now becoming popular, mostly due to the positive results turf scientists and the more organically minded homeowners have achieved with it. A good manual on the subject is needed to help communicate the basic ideas and procedures, and to that end I have written this book. When you are finished reading it, I hope you will see lawn care in a new light. And I hope you will understand just how simple lawn care can be—naturally!

In the few years since the first release of this book, we've seen environmental concern grow to become part of everyday life. This concern **is** affecting lawn research and the products that are appearing on the market. **A healthy lawn is an environmental healer.** It will help clean our atmosphere, purify our rain water, prevent erosion, buffer noise, and cool our air in the summer. But the methods we've used to care for our lawns in the past have offset some of the good that lawns do. This book was originally written to show the homeowner, and those in the lawn care industry, how to build and maintain a healthy lawn, without harm to our environment. Today, it can be done easily.

1 ◆ WHAT IS A LAWN?

A lawn is simply an area of land covered with one or more types of turf grasses. In a typical 25-by-40-foot section (1000 square feet), there are about one million grass plants. These grasses are usually low growing, deep green, and durable. Some types grow best in the heat, and others can't tolerate it. Some types are fine, or narrow-bladed. Others are coarse, or thick-bladed. All types are capable of forming the green carpeting of the earth we have come to call a lawn.

HOW GRASS GROWS

This is a very simplified drawing of a grass plant, which we'll use for illustrative purposes. A clear understanding of each part discussed will greatly enhance your ability to create a healthy lawn.

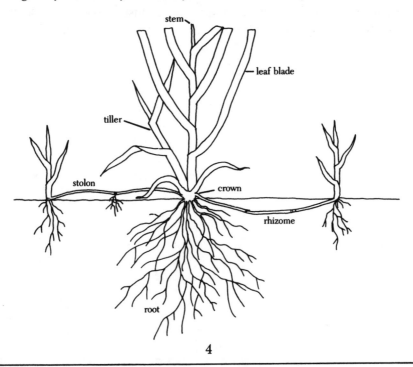

The part the homeowner is most familiar with is the leaf blade. On closer inspection you will find that the leaf actually rolls itself tightly around the shoot (or stem), forming the **leaf sheath**.

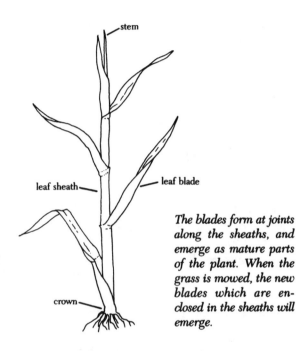

The blades form at joints along the sheaths, and emerge as mature parts of the plant. When the grass is mowed, the new blades which are enclosed in the sheaths will emerge.

The stems and leaves all emanate, or grow out from, the **crown** area of the plant. The crown is located at or near the ground surface, and is the main growth center for the aboveground parts of the grass plant. The activity that goes on in the crown makes grass different from all other plants. Other types of plants grow at their outer extremities, or tips, and must be pruned or trimmed very carefully. But grass grows from its base. This means that you can mow the tips off without harming the plant.

The roots of the grass plant grow in a more typical fashion. New cells form at the tips of the roots, not at the base. The roots grow in search of water and nutritive substances. Tiny root hairs form to take these in. If the tips of the roots are damaged or allowed to dry out, the actual point of growth is injured and recovery is not easy.

In the first drawing of the grass plant, notice how deep and full the roots of the mother plant are. Most grasses develop more and more

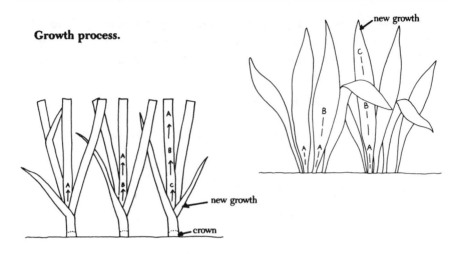

Growth process.

new growth

new growth

crown

roots if the lawn is allowed to grow higher. These deeper roots seek out water and nutrients. Shortly cropped grass, on the other hand, will have shorter roots, and therefore need more water and extra nutrients to compensate for what they can't get for themselves. Topgrowth and roots are mutually supportive: they balance each other out in the quantity, or bulk (not length), of each. If that balance is upset for too long a period, the grass will suffer.

HOW GRASS SPREADS

There are four methods grass plants normally use to spread themselves, and most species are capable of two or more of these. The first method is by **going to seed**. At certain times during the growing season, a grass plant might begin to form flowers, and then seeds, atop the flower stalks. If the grass is not mowed short enough to chop these seed heads off, the seeds will mature, drop to the ground, and perhaps become new grass plants.

Another way grass plants spread is by adding new shoots to the original plant. These new shoots are called **tillers**. (See grass plant drawing.)

Tillers rise from the crown and thicken the original grass plant. Many grasses add on tillers, but some use this method almost exclusively to spread out. Grasses of this nature are called bunch, or clump, grasses. Tall fescue is a very common bunch grass.

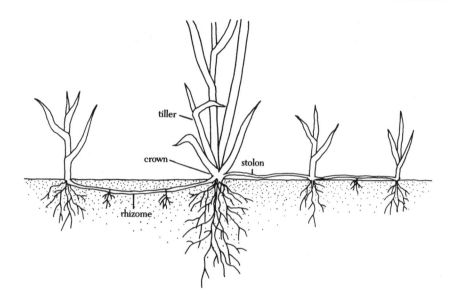

Looking back at our original grass plant drawing, you will see that there are two daughter plants that have come from the mother plant. The shoot or stem that connects them to the mother plant also originates in the crown. When the stem travels under the soil surface, it is called a **rhizome**. Kentucky bluegrass spreads by rhizomes, which can travel quite a distance to an open spot in the lawn, or into the loose fertile soil of your flower beds.

When a plant spreads by an aboveground stem, that stem is called a **stolon**. Many of the southern grasses spread across a lawn by vigorous stolon growth. Stolon-type grasses, such as St. Augustinegrass, tend to choke out weeds and other lawn grasses.

HOW A LAWN GETS ITS FOOD

Most people think that the roots take in food from the soil, and then the grass plant uses that food to produce leaf blades. This single misconception results in more ruined lawns than anything else. It leads to poor watering, mowing, and fertilizing practices—surefire ways to ruin a lawn.

The truth of the matter is that *a grass plant manufactures its own food in its leaf blades.*

Does that make sense? Of course it does. That is what photosynthesis is all about. Remember that term from grade school?

Photosynthesis

Photo means "light"; *synthesis* means "a putting together." Green plants use sunlight to put together, or make, the food they need for proper growth and health. Here's how it works:

The sun's energy is the key. It helps the leaves turn carbon dioxide (from the air) into sugars (food). The sugars can then be broken down and combined into fats, proteins, and other necessary building blocks for plant life.

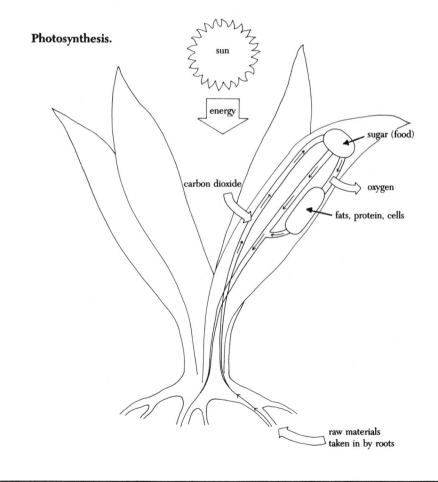

Photosynthesis.

The roots, meanwhile, gather the raw materials and water that help make photosynthesis possible. The roots also bring in the minerals and nutrients that are used for functions other than photosynthesis. Fertilizers provide many nutrients and raw materials that help a plant make food, but fertilizer itself is not food.

Let's review this, because it is important to know the basics.

1. The roots take in raw materials and water.
2. These raw materials travel up to the leaf blades where they are converted into food.
3. The sun's energy is needed to make this process (called photosynthesis) possible.
4. The food that is made (sugars) builds most of the different types of cells that the plant needs for the continuous growth of stems, leaf blades, and roots.

When a lawn isn't cut too short, and has plenty of leaf blade exposed to the sun, each grass plant will produce the cells and energy needed for more and taller leaf blades and deeper, stronger roots.

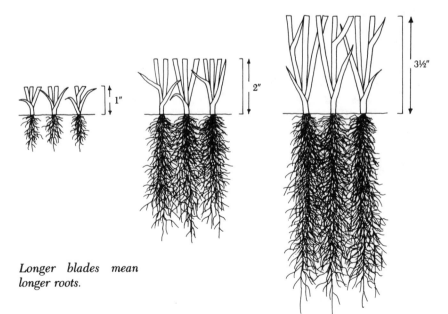

Longer blades mean longer roots.

The deeper the roots, the greater the capability of finding nutrients (especially in poor soils) and of withstanding drought. Deep roots not only reach a deeper water supply, but store food during times when the top isn't growing.

Balance

Let's get back to the idea of the balance of root and leaf blade. If some of the root were to be cut off due to insect damage, the leaf blades' source of water and nutrients would be diminished. The plant would wither and perhaps die.

This can also happen when a shallow-rooted lawn gets dried out in the top couple inches of soil. The leaf blades can't get the raw materials they need for photosynthesis, and soon don't have enough energy to support themselves. They wither up, attempting to conserve moisture, and die quickly. If the grass plant has been healthy, with deep roots and plenty of nutrients in root storage, it will simply go dormant (inactive) until the drought is over.

How about the other side of the coin? Let's say the grass blades, not the roots, have been cut too short. Now the photosynthesizing food factory in the blades has been removed. The thick root network, which needs energy to gather nutrients and water, and to maintain itself, has just lost its food supply. All its stored food must go quickly to the top for leaf development and photosynthesis. If there is not enough stored food to keep the plant alive while the leaf blade is regrowing, the grass will die. If there is enough, the grass will survive, but while this emergency is being handled you can expect some of the roots to die off from lack of food. With continued short cropping of the lawn, the grass won't have a chance to recover.

For many grass types, a proper balance between root and top growth is the key to health. Without it, no amount of fertilizing, spraying, or watering will make your lawn healthy.

2 ♦ MOWING

The very least you must do for a lawn is mow it. In fact, many of you will not do anything more for your lawn than that. Fine. You can have a nicer-looking lawn in a matter of weeks simply by changing your mowing practices. But you will need an understanding of what is going on.

Always make sure your lawn is standing straight. From the previous chapter, you know that the leaf blades must be exposed to sunlight. This is why lawn grasses should not get too high: above three or four inches they tend to lean over and block sunlight. Long, trampled grass also tends to mat up. There is an attachment available for some mowers that runs tines ahead of the cutting blade and helps to lift up matted grass. **A light raking in the opposite direction of the way the lawn is leaning** will make the lawn stand straighter and cut better. It will help get rid of matting, and will clean and invigorate the lawn as well. The common rotary mower (with a horizontally spinning flat blade) creates a vacuum when run at higher speeds that lifts the grass straight before cutting it.

If your raking pulls up lengths of sideways-growing grass in an otherwise upright lawn, you may have **bentgrass**, a problem for most homeowners in the northern or cool-weather states. Bentgrass especially should be kept upright if it is in the lawn, or it will spread and create unsightly patches, or **colonies**. Bentgrass and other similar low-growing types of grasses are cut differently, and will be discussed later in the book. Most of the lawn grasses we're concerned with are the upright-growing types.

HOW HIGH TO CUT

This is simple to figure out. You must keep an upright grass relatively long so that it will have the food and energy necessary for healthy development, top and bottom. But the blades must stand up firmly so that the lawn will not only look good, but won't mat up and

11

prevent the flow of air and moisture, and the penetration of light. The proper height for most lawn grasses is higher than most of you are probably cutting now.

Don't worry that your lawn will look unkempt. *It is how even the grass is, not how high it is, that makes a lawn look good.* And contrary to popular opinion, you'll need to cut a taller lawn less often than you would if you kept it short. Taller grass gives the additional benefit of shading out many types of sun-loving weeds.

Different grasses are cut at different heights, and grass types vary across the country depending on climate and growing conditions. A state such as California runs the gamut of the various grass types due to its vast differences east to west and north to south. (See *Lawn Grasses by Climate* map, page 83.)

Don't just mechanically follow a chart to measure how high to cut your lawn, since you're dealing both with living things and with environmental factors. You must see the grass in front of you, not the lawn on the cover of this book. Many conditions can affect how high you cut your lawn.

A general rule to follow is **never cut off more than one-third of the blade at once.** This will keep the grass from losing too much of its food factory and going into shock.

CUT GRASS WHEN IT'S DRY

A dry lawn stands up straighter and gives a cleaner cut. It is less messy, too. If the grass blades don't seem to want to dry out, you might have a problem with inadequate air flow in your yard, or too much shade. If neither of these are the problem, cut the grass a little shorter to allow more sun and air to penetrate. Soil that stays moist is a totally different problem, to be discussed later. It should be noted here that **shaded lawns should normally be cut a little higher than those in full sun, to make up for lack of sunlight.**

MODIFY CUTTING HEIGHTS BY SEASON

The height at which you cut your lawn depends on how the grass is growing at that particular time. By season, here's what I usually do on a common northern lawn in areas of ample yearly rainfall. In the early spring the grass relies on the food stored in its roots to start it growing again. First comes spring clean-up which means raking debris off the lawn and lifting any matted grass.

I make my first cut short. This cuts away some of the dead grass left from the previous season, invigorates and stimulates the lawn, allows more sunlight to reach the newly forming blades, and helps to heat the soil. **I then raise the mower height to about two inches and leave it there for a couple of cuts**, or until the entire lawn has started to grow vigorously. Cutting at this height encourages the grass to thicken up by growing new tillers that add on to the mother plant. It also encourages stolons and rhizomes.

When the grass really starts to take off, I let it reach 3–4 inches in height, and keep it there. By keeping it high, even in the spring when there is plenty of water and food available from root storage, you can crowd out many potential weeds, especially crab-grass. If you had a weak lawn last season, or one with shallow roots that didn't store much over the winter, yet survived, it might take a little longer to attain a 3- to 4-inch height. Don't cut down to the weaker grass's height. Cut high, and encourage the blades to grow and produce a healthier plant.

Sometimes a little fertilizer is necessary to stimulate a weak section of grass. Fertilize *early* in the spring so the grass can build up its strength and gain height before the summer heat comes on. A healthy lawn won't need early spring fertilizing; it will take off on its own. The general principle you should follow is this:

A weak plant needs to have more leaf blades to produce the food and energy it needs to regain its health.

SUMMER MOWING

In midsummer the northern lawn should be kept high. It will provide its own shade and won't need much cutting unless you water it deeply and often. The northern grasses thrive in late spring and early fall weather. If the grass is healthy when summer approaches, it will naturally go dormant and turn brown. In a dormant lawn the activity above ground shuts down until more water becomes available. Grass should still be left high during this period. The shade it casts on the ground, as well as its thickness, will keep weeds from taking over. Tall blades will prevent some evaporation and make recovery easier.

A lawn won't go dormant during a wet, cool summer, or if it has been kept watered throughout a dry, hot summer. It is fine to keep the grass watered during a dry spell if the watering is done properly and the blades are fairly long. However, the cool-season grasses in the northern areas don't thrive in extreme heat. If the temperature is consistently high, you will have a hard time keeping the grass from going dormant, even if you water. Shaded lawns will be easier to keep green.

Some people think that if they let their grass turn brown it will die. That, of course, isn't usually the case; the grass will simply go dormant. It should recover easily when the rains begin again, because it has food stored in its roots.

If a lawn doesn't recover after a dry period (and it isn't being weakened by insects or disease), it was a weak lawn to begin with—probably because it was cut too short. The grass was unable to store any food in its roots, since it used up all its food just to stay alive.

At the end of a dry summer, when the rain comes again, dormant grass greens up very quickly, much the way it did in the springtime. It uses root-stored food to get it going again.

I keep the lawn high well into the fall. This is very important. During early and mid-fall the grass will be replenishing its store of food in the roots. Northern grasses will continue to grow (slowly) until temperatures consistently remain below freezing.

As the weather begins to cool and leaves fall from the trees, you'll notice that the grass's growth rate is slowing down. You won't have to cut as often. **This is your signal to start lowering the cutting height.** Be sure to do this very gradually, and don't go below 1½ inches. The green color tells you that photosynthesis is still at work. The food is going mostly to the roots for storage at this time, and is not being wasted on blade growth. The grass should look green even after you cut it. If it looks slightly yellow, you've cut it too short. Continue to cut at 1½ inches until the grass stops growing entirely. Your lawn should still be green when you put your mower away for the winter. As long as the grass is green it is producing food and sending it to the roots for storage. When the ground freezes or gets covered with snow, the grass will go dormant and take on a brown tinge. But with a few warm days of winter thaw, it will green up again and photosynthesis will begin anew. Be sure to keep leaves and debris off the lawn over the winter so the sun can reach the grass. This will also prevent smothering and rotting.

SOUTHERN LAWNS

The difference between the warm-season grasses of the South and the cool-season grasses of the North is that the warm-season grasses take off when the temperatures are high. They grow slowly during spring and fall, which is when the cool-season grasses thrive. During the winter, even if temperatures remain far above freezing most of the time, the warm-season grasses go dormant and turn brown. (Many weeds, however, enjoy these somewhat cool temperatures.) A common practice in the South is to plant a wintergrass right over a lawn just as winter begins and the lawn starts to go dormant. The wintergrass is simply a quick-growing, cool-season grass type (usually annual ryegrass) that will stay green over the winter and keep weeds out. It will die back or get choked out by early summer. (More about wintergrass in a later chapter.)

There are greater differences among grasses of the South than those of the North (temperature, humidity, and soil differences demand this variety) so it is not practical to describe a general seasonal plan. The Bermudagrasses, which are the most common of the warm-season grasses, don't do well with high mowing. You can set the mower at 1½–2 inches and keep it there all season and have a nice, fine-bladed lawn. Some varieties are cut at half an inch and can be used for the fanciest of lawns.

The thicker-bladed grasses, such as St. Augustine's and many low-maintenance coastal grasses, are cut at 2–3, and even 4 inches throughout their growing season. Many spread by aboveground stolons and need most frequent cutting during midsummer. The height of the southern grasses should be lowered gradually in the fall if you plan to plant a wintergrass. If not, don't cut too short or you'll be making room for weeds.

WHEN TO CUT

Each time you cut you slice off part of the grass plants' food factory. This is a shock to your lawn, and the more you cut off, the greater the shock will be. Many people let their lawns get much too high before cutting, and consequently put unnecessary strain on the grass as well as the mower. In general, **during periods of quick growth you shouldn't cut off more than one third of the total**

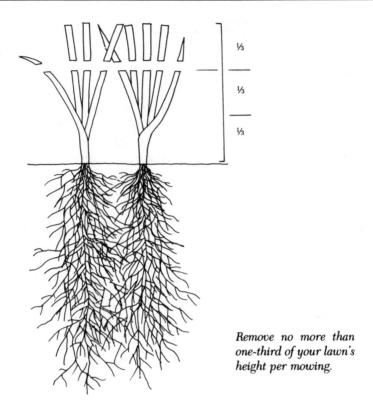

⅓

⅓

⅓

*Remove no more than
one-third of your lawn's
height per mowing.*

height of the grass, preferably less. That is about as much as the
grass can easily withstand. If you are trying to maintain a grass height
of 3 inches, wait until the grass reaches 4–4½ inches before cutting,
provided it is growing quickly. If the growth has slowed down, then
I'd try to take off less at each cutting. Since the grass is growing
slower, its recuperative powers are diminished. Try to create as little
shock as possible.

The homeowner has a distinct advantage over a lawn-cutting service. He or she can cut the grass as often as necessary, each time at
the proper height. Lawn-cutting services usually come once a week
and might have to cut nearly half the leaf blade, especially in the
spring (or the summer in the South), to bring the grass down to the
correct height. A lawn usually survives this kind of treatment if it has
favorable growing conditions, but it might look pretty shaggy while
waiting for that cutting.

THE NEGLECTED LAWN

If you are faced with a neglected lawn that has grown 6–8 inches tall, the proper treatment is to mow it in stages. Cut an 8-inch lawn down to 6 inches. Wait a few days while the grass recuperates, then cut it to 4 inches. Wait again and then cut it to 3 inches. Cutting an 8-inch lawn right down to 3 inches creates too much of a shock. There will be no green left on the blades, which means no food factory. The grass could easily die or become weak and fall prey to insects and disease. Cutting at a 6-inch height might involve the rental of a high-wheel mower. Most homeowner models won't cut above 3½–4 inches, and the movement in the industry is to lower that height even more because too many careless people have slid their feet under mowers. So be extra careful whenever you mow at the higher settings, and check for hidden stones and debris before beginning.

GRASS TYPES ARE DIFFERENT

There are only a few common grass varieties that can survive very low cutting. If your neighbor has a putting green type of lawn, he probably has a putting green type of grass. That type of lawn requires a lot more watering, fertilizing, mowing, and disease control than a normal lawn does. As you can figure out for yourself, the lack of leaf blade surface on these short lawns means a weaker plant that must be pampered in order to survive.

The lushest, greenest stands of grass you see in front lawns are rarely short, especially in the North. Look for yourself this summer. Your neighbor who keeps her lawn relatively high will have a green lawn with little care. But the neighbor who tries to have a fancy, short lawn, without the right type of grass, will have difficulty keeping her lawn nice and green. She'll be watering and fertilizing a lot more than she should have to.

Another unworkable idea I've heard from many homeowners is that if they cut their grass short, they'll have to mow it less often. This is not necessarily true (unless they are scalping the lawn). Mowing short will encourage the grass to grow faster in order to replace lost leaf blades. If kept short for too long, however, the grass will weaken as it uses up its stored energy supply. Then recovery from the short cutting will be slow. The weakened grass will be susceptible to insects, weeds, disease, and ultimately, destruction.

The chart below will provide a *rough* guide to mowing heights for common lawn grasses. The height refers to the *actual length of grass*—not just the setting on your mower. Mowers can sink into a lawn and cut too short or ride on top of a lawn and cut too long, depending on numerous factors (mower weight, tire width, degree of soil compaction, soil moisture, thatch, type of grass). This is an important point that is usually overlooked, even by the professional mowing services.

WHAT ABOUT GRASS CLIPPINGS?

Grass clippings are almost 80 percent water; another 10 percent is mostly fiber. What is left over happens to be those same elements that are found in a balanced fertilizer. In theory, then, if you were to leave all your clippings to decompose on the lawn, you would never have to fertilize, because you would simply be recycling the grass continually. Whenever you remove the clippings from a lawn you are disrupting the natural cycle of growth and decomposition. You are removing nutrients which must somehow be replaced, or the lawn will deteriorate. If you regularly remove clippings, you *must* fertilize to replace the lost nutrients (see chapter 6, *Fertilizing*). Not all the nutrients stay in the soil, however, due to **leaching** (rain or irrigation washing substances down too deep into the soil to be of use), and some loss through gases formed during decomposition.

Many lawns stay green and healthy without being fertilized. Now you may be saying to yourself "I'm never going to fertilize again . . . I'll just leave the grass clippings on the lawn and let them recycle." Hold on! Before you act on that decision there are certain adjustments to make and factors to consider.

First, the clippings must be short enough so that they do not mat down on top of the lawn. They should filter down to the soil level and quickly decompose. *Cut often* or the clippings will be too long—they'll mat up on top of the lawn and choke out the grass. If the clippings are long you could try mowing over them again to help disperse them. The usual procedure is to catch the clippings and throw them back onto the lawn, but if the grass was too high or too damp when you cut it, the clippings will leave unsightly clumps. I'll

APPROXIMATE CUTTING HEIGHTS

Grass Name	Type	Height in Inches
Northern Grasses		
Bentgrass	Creeping	¼–1
	Colonial	½–1¼
Fescue	Red	2–4
	Chewing	1½–3
	Tall	3–5
Kentucky Bluegrass	Common	2–4
	Improved	1½–4
Ryegrass	Perennial	1½–3½
	Annual	1½–3½
Turf-type Tall Fescue	Improved	2–4
Zoysiagrass	(limited use in North)	½–2
Southern Grasses		
Bahiagrass		2½–4
Bermudagrass	Common	½–1½
	Improved	¼–1
Carpetgrass		1½–2½
Centipedegrass		1½–2½
St. Augustinegrass		2–4
Zoysiagrass		½–2
Native grasses—more common in harsher and dryer climates		
Buffalograss		1–2½
Wheatgrass (Agropyron)		2–4

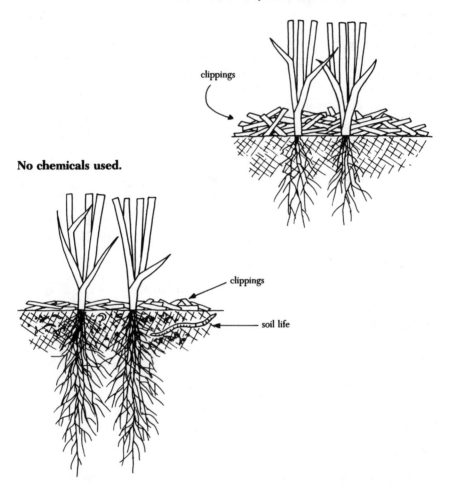

Chemically treated lawn.

clippings

No chemicals used.

clippings

soil life

repeat what I said before: *see the lawn in front of you*. There are too many variables to be able to rely entirely on some chart in a book. If you understand the ideas in this book, you'll know when and how high to cut, and long or damp clippings won't be a problem.

The second factor to take into account regarding lawn clippings is that *on over-chemicalized lawns, clippings may not decompose as quickly as on chemical-free lawns*. This problem will be covered in much more detail later. For now I'll say that certain chemicals kill off the bacteria and microbes that aid decomposition, and make worms, the soil's intestines, scarce or nonexistent. I would catch or rake up the grass clippings on a once over-chemicalized lawn until the life in the soil is restored. The way to go about restoring soil life will also be covered in a later section.

The third factor concerning grass clippings is **thatch**. Thatch is a matted layer of grass stems, roots, clippings, and runners that sits on top of the soil. *Grass clippings will not cause thatch unless they mat up without decomposing.* In fact, most of the thatch problems I've handled over the years were on lawns where the clippings were always caught in the mower's bag. Clippings will add to thatch, however, if the condition already exists. You should be able to slip your finger down through the grass and touch the soil. If your finger gets caught up in a mat of thatch more than half an inch deep, I'd start removing the clippings and concentrate on handling the thatch. (See chapter 7, *Thatch.*)

Mulching Mowers

As I mentioned earlier, mulching mowers chop up the grass clippings finely and throw them back onto the lawn. You should be able to use them on any lawn that is cut two inches or higher. Except in situations when the grass is too high or wet to mulch properly, or when clippings aren't desired at all, these mowers are ideal. Many of today's mowers have a mulching attachment that you can purchase. It is worth the additional expense.

HOW TO CUT

1. Keep your lawn mower blades sharp and you will always make a clean cut. The effect of a dull blade is easy to detect: the top surface of your lawn will look gray or white because the grass blades have been torn or ripped instead of sliced. This type of mowing exposes a wounded grass blade to insect and disease organisms. It creates extra stress, since the plant must repair these tears before growing. So start the season with sharp blades and never let them get dull. Torn grass tips recover slowly, especially in midsummer when the grass is most susceptible to damage. For larger lawns, sharpen your blades more often, and keep an extra blade on hand (for rotary mowers) so you can mow the lawn while the other blade is being sharpened.

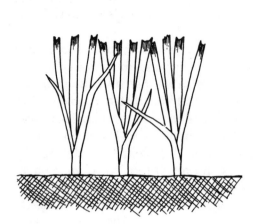

A dull mower blade rips rather than slices the grass.

Even the best of us hit a root or stone now and then. File the nicks out right away, before they get worse. Balance the blades when you sharpen them (or have them sharpened) so one side isn't lighter than the other. An unbalanced blade makes a poor cut, and strains the mower, too.

Reel mowers usually have at least five blades, which are of higher-quality metal than rotary blades. They cut with a scissorlike action, giving a cleaner cut than rotary blades do. They need sharpening less frequently, but must be brought to a shop for sharpening on a special machine (which means more cost to the customer). If you allow your reel blades to get dull, they will shred the grass and strain the engine, just as dull rotary blades will.

2. Keep the underside of the cutting deck clean. Wet grass will clump up there, especially on rotary mowers, and won't allow the grass to lift up as the mower passes over it, resulting in a poor cut. Clean before each mowing, using a putty knife or a flat stick. Please disconnect the spark plug first, move the mower off the grass, and wear gloves so you won't slice yourself on the blade. I should add that when you turn your mower on its side to clean it, make sure gas or oil doesn't pour out the top. Refer to your owner's manual if you have one.

3. Keep the discharge shoot unclogged so the clippings can shoot out easily. Damp grass, or too much grass cut at once, will clog up the shoot, especially if there is a grass catcher set-up. *Never* put your hand inside or near the chute when the mower is running.

4. Do not add gas or oil to your mower while it's on the lawn. If you miss your target you will kill the lawn in that spot. Check your oil and gas *before* you start to mow.

5. Before you begin to cut your lawn, take a quick look to see if there are any stones or sticks around. Aside from dulling the blade, stones fly out of the grass shoot and damage whatever they hit, people included. It is also possible for a hard object to wedge itself between the blades and the mower deck. This could bend the blades, and even ruin the main works of the engine.

6. Know your mower—in particular where the blades are in relation to the deck and the wheels. This way you can safely direct the mower around tree roots and vent pipes, and you will not scalp your lawn, especially where it meets a walk. Use common sense and you can keep the tougher sections of terrain cut safely.

7. Alternate your mowing pattern frequently. Cutting exactly the same way each time can lead to waves and tire ruts in the lawn. The grass tends to lean in one direction or another after cutting, so by alternating your pattern you'll encourage the grass to stand upright. An upright lawn gives a better cut. If your lawn isn't very upright, a stiff raking in the opposite direction of wherever it is leaning (before cutting) should handle the problem. If your mower comes equipped with a raking or dethatching attachment that is meant to be used when mowing, by all means use it.

8. Watch where the clippings are going. If you have a rotary mower with a side discharge chute, you must control where the clippings are going to land. There are two reasons for this. The first is to avoid blowing grass, grass seeds, and weed seeds into flower beds or other places where you don't want them. The second reason is that you can create a buildup of grass clippings on the lawn that will be too thick to mow over.

The simplest way to mow your lawn is to go around the perimeter, working your way inward with the chute pointed outward. If you have beds around your lawn, mow the opposite way (blowing the clippings inward) until it's safe to turn the mower around. Because you should be changing your mowing patterns frequently, you'll have to do a little thinking beforehand to make sure the grass clippings go where you want them to.

Scalping.

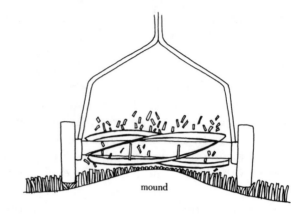

mound

Scalping.

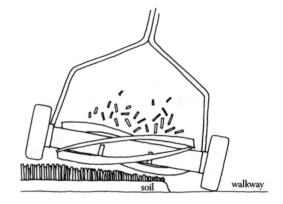

soil   walkway

Correct.

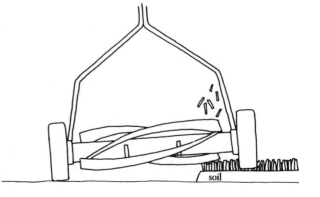

soil

9. Keep your lines straight when mowing. Give your lawn a neat appearance by keeping the mower moving in a straight line, rather than wiggling all over the lawn. Your tires will usually leave a slight depression in the grass. Don't run the tires in the same groove on the way back—overlap to the inside to make sure you don't miss any grass.

10. Don't push your mower too hard if you run into thicker, wetter, or tougher grass. Slow down a bit; hesitate over that section to make sure the grass gets cut. If you are mowing a thick lawn that is straining the engine, try cutting only half the width of the mower with each pass.

11. Cut hills or steep grades very carefully, or don't mow them at all. A common mowing accident is slipping on a hill and having a foot go under the mower, especially in wet conditions. If the slope is too steep to mow, try planting a ground cover over it. On a gentle slope either push the mower up the grade or across it—*if* it is dry. You're looking for trouble if you try to control a mower going downhill.

12. Don't allow children to mow a lawn until they are physically strong enough to control the mower, and responsible enough to understand these mowing tips.

3♦CHOOSING YOUR LAWN EQUIPMENT

LAWN MOWERS

Homeowners often ask me to recommend a mower for them to buy. There are many choices with all sorts of options and attachments, but what I want most is a dependable machine that starts every time and does a good job with little maintenance or repair. For this reason I suggest you **buy a name-brand mower from a dealer who can supply parts and service**. Go to a store that specializes in lawn equipment and get to know the people there. You are more likely to come away with the right machine for your needs, as well as better service than you would receive from a non-specialty store. When you bring your machine in for service or repairs, the lawn equipment dealer will be more responsive to one of "his" machines, and he'll want to assure your future business.

Reel vs. Rotary

Most of the mowers sold today are rotaries. These have a horizontal blade which spins at tremendous speed, creating a slight vacuum to lift the grass before cutting it. The blade hits the grass and slices it, much the way a scythe would.

Reel mowers consist of five or more slightly curved blades turning on a horizontal cylinder. At the bottom of the mower is a flat cutter bar. This bar pushes the grass slightly forward until the blade swings against it and slices it the way a pair of scissors would.

This cut is a lot cleaner than a rotary cut. Putting greens and short, manicured lawns are always cut with reel mowers.

Reel mowers should not be used on tall or tough-bladed lawns. They don't have the necessary speed or strength, and their cutting height is rarely adjustable above two inches. The rotary's blade hits with high impact, and with a strong engine can cut through any type of lawn grass. You will, however, see more frayed grass tips on a rotary-cut lawn. This is because rotary cutting is less precise, and

26

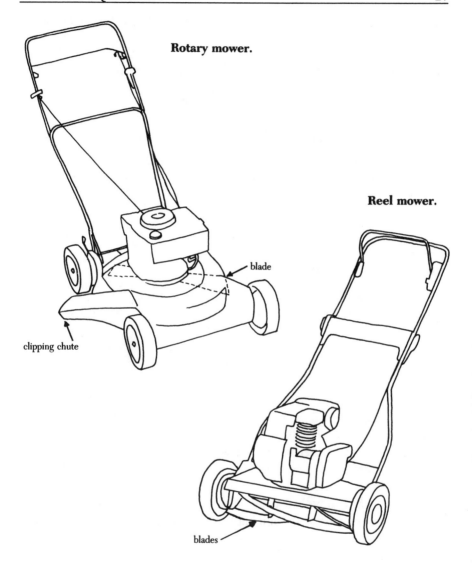

Rotary mower.

Reel mower.

blade

clipping chute

blades

because a rotary mower's fast-moving blade dulls sooner than a reel mower's.

The rotary mower rides on four wheels and, if the operator is careful, can cut bumpy lawns without much damage. Because the reel mower rides on just two wheels, it is more vulnerable to rough spots in the terrain. When a wheel drops into a dip, the whole mower follows it, and the lawn gets scalped. And because the reel spins rather slowly, it will jam up if it hits a small mound or catches a twig.

The popularity of rotary mowers has put homeowner reel mowers on the endangered species list. You can still purchase a push-type reel mower with no motor on it, and if you have a small, short, fine-bladed lawn, this simple machine will serve you well. Motorized reel mowers are much harder to find, and they are costly. A good one runs $500–$600 (as of 1988) and up. Options include electric start, self-propelling, and grass catchers. Greenskeeper models, in case you're wondering, go for $1500.

Electric Rotary Mowers

Rotary mowers come in a wide choice of styles, options, and attachments. Electric rotaries are quite common, and for good reason. They are much lighter than gas-powered mowers, require no gas refills or oil changes, and no engine maintenance. They start immediately, run quieter, and don't pollute the air. Keep the top and underside clean, and the blade sharp, and they'll be fine.

On the down side, when you mow with an electric you have to drag a power cord around, and refrain from cutting it. You must devise a cutting pattern that requires the least fiddling with the cord. Electric mowers are less powerful than gas mowers—usually no more than three horsepower—which makes cutting a tall, thick, or slightly damp grass difficult. Cutting a damp lawn is never good practice, but cutting one with an electric mower could be dangerous. The mower itself is built to be pretty safe around moisture, but the cord might have a nick in it, which could lead to a shocking experience!

Gasoline-Powered Rotary Mowers

Since gasoline-powered rotary mowers have no cord to pull around, they afford you much more mobility than electric types. They also have more power. I recommend a 3.5 horsepower mower for a normal lawn. If the mower is self-propelled it should have 4 horsepower. The more horsepower, the less strain on the engine, and the greater its ability to cut and throw grass. The bigger the pricetag, too.

All Engines Are Not Created Equal

All lawnmower engines look pretty much the same on the outside, but on the inside there is a wide range of quality among models. Even two engines from the same manufacturer and of the same horsepower can be very different. By substituting parts made with weaker materials or smaller sizes, manufacturers create light-duty engines out of heavy-duty ones. Installing light-duty engines, as well as light-duty parts, on a mower is one way to build a "discount" model—and we all know what discount usually means. Don't be fooled just because you see a familiar name on the engine.

The folks at a good mower shop will know about engine strengths, and should be able to offer you a broad selection of quality machines. To make sure you get a tough engine, consider purchasing a machine with an I/C (industrial/commercial) engine. It might cost an extra fifty to seventy-five dollars, but under normal use it will probably last five years longer than a cheaper machine.

The newest development in mowers is the overhead valve engine. This type of engine can run at a lower speed and produce more power, so it should last longer. It requires very little maintenance, and starts easily with a pull-cord.

The BBC

The BBC (blade-brake clutch) is a safety feature which you'll find on new mowers. When you pull it, it engages the blade and starts it spinning. When you let go of the BBC, the blade stops within three seconds, but the engine keeps running. This feature allows you to empty a grass catcher or pick up sticks or lawn debris without shutting off the engine. An additional benefit of the BBC is that you can start the engine with the blade disengaged. It's safer and easier that way.

MOWER MAINTENANCE

1. Keep the air filter clean! This point cannot be overemphasized. Almost all the dirt that the carburetor sucks in should be caught by the air filter. If the filter gets clogged it will allow dirt to get into the engine and wear down vital parts. Clogged air filters will also rob the carburetor of air, causing starting problems and poor engine performance.

Most air filters are made of a tough paper. If they can't be cleaned with an air hose or brush, they should be replaced. You will usually find a spongelike air cleaner surrounding the filter. This should be washed regularly with a mild detergent, and rinsed well. After it dries, dribble on a tablespoon of clean oil and work it in. The air cleaner should feel lightly saturated.

2. Keep the oil clean and full. Start with lightweight oil in the spring and change it at least once during the season (commercial outfits should change it weekly). A good amount of dirt in the engine ends up in the oil. Furthermore, oil breaks down after awhile and loses its lubricating qualities. Use the proper weight oil, recommended by your owner's manual. If you don't have a manual, straight 30 weight oil is your best bet. Check your oil level before you begin mowing, and never let it get too low. Without proper lubrication the engine will seize-up, and you can kiss it goodbye.

3. Use fresh gas. After sitting around for a month or more, gas begins to break down. Part of it turns gummy, and this can wreak havoc on the carburetor. Old gas might also have water in it from condensation. Water settles to the bottom of the gas tank and can cause poor starting or running—or no running at all.

Winter Care

When you approach your final cuts of the season, get stingy on the gas. After your last cut you should drain the tank completely, and there is no point in ending up with a full tank to drain. After you drain the tank, start the mower up if you can to clean out the fuel lines and carburetor. A varnish-like film will form on the carburetor if gas sits in it all winter.

Drain and replace the engine oil now, while the engine is still warm. It will flow easier that way. Remove the spark plug, squirt in ten to fifteen drops of lubricating oil, and crank the engine over a few times to distribute this oil inside the engine. Clean and regap the spark plug, or replace it.

Sharpen the blade and, wearing gloves, rub it with a rag dipped in your old oil. This will prevent rust (and the gloves will keep poisonous used motor oil away from your skin). In fact, you should do this to all exposed bare metal on the mower. Grease any moving parts, clean the mower up, and you will be ready for the spring. In my business we follow these simple maintenance procedures and are able to take a 4 horsepower mower, with an overhead valve I/C engine, through the equivalent of forty years of homeowner use.

OTHER MOWER FEATURES

- **Grass catchers.** When I want to catch my clippings, a rear-bagging mower is my first choice. Rear bags hold more than side bags; they don't clog as often at the discharge chute; and they don't hang out to the side, demanding emergency maneuvers to avoid trees, walls, and other obstacles.
- **Heavy-duty wheels.** Try to find a mower with wide wheels. They cause less compaction and less visible tire grooves when you mow. Steel wheels can take plenty of the twisting that goes with mowing, while plastic wheels often snap off at the axle. Plastic wheels, however, are less expensive. For home use, make tire width more of a priority.
- **Starters.** Electric-start mowers are more expensive, though convenient. Since they are more complex machines they are more likely to need repairs somewhere down the line. If you are considering electric start only because you've had poor experience with pull-start engines, try an overhead valve engine mower. If an engine doesn't want to start with a pull-cord, it won't start with a key, either.
- **Self-propelled mowers.** On larger lawns without a lot of corners or tight spots, a self-propelled mower makes mowing less of a chore. Most lawns have sections that are best done without the SP (self-propelling) unit on, so make sure the mower you buy can be pushed manually. And because the same engine that powers the blade must power the SP mechanism, make sure the engine is strong—at least 4 horsepower.

   For the most part, I prefer to mow without the SP on. I can feel the grass being cut and make slight hesitations when the grass is thick or tougher to mow. With the SP on, I tend to mow too quickly for the best cut. So make sure there is a wide range of speed settings on the SP unit if you want one. And see that the driving gears or chains are not exposed on the deck or front axle. This kind of set-up, found on many less expensive mowers, is extremely susceptible to damage when you bump into branches and other snares.

- **Riding mowers.** These are a must for large-acreage lawns. Not only do they save you from exhaustion, but they cut in a wider swath than most walk-behind mowers do. Riders are quite heavy, especially with someone sitting on them, so you must avoid mowing until the ground is dry or you'll leave tire ruts. You normally can't get close to borders, buildings, or trees on a rider. Follow-up mowing with a push mower, or trimming with a string trimmer, is usually necessary.

   Riding mowers are fun to use, but they are not toys. Try to keep your enthusiasm under control. Giving your kids rides on them, even with the blades turned off, can be dangerous.

- **Mulching mowers.** Only a few companies manufacture mulching mowers. These machines cut the grass, chop it up a bit, and toss it back onto the lawn, hopefully in an unnoticeable condition. Because the clippings are chopped up, they should decompose faster than clippings thrown out of a grass chute. A mulching mower will enhance the health and beauty of a medium-to-tall lawn. However, as mentioned in the section on grass clippings, you can't use a mulcher all the time. For that reason the mower should be able to adjust to a side-chute discharge, or it should have a bagging set-up. It might be more sensible to find a regular mower that offers a mulching attachment.

Attachments

- **Mulcher.** As I have just mentioned, some lawn mowers may be equipped with a mulching attachment. It is usually placed on the discharge chute or under the deck. If it works correctly, the clippings will be chopped up and will recycle themselves faster.
- **Side-discharge chute** (for rear-bagging mowers). After reading this book you might decide to leave your clippings on the lawn instead of catching them. If you have a rear-bagging mower you can't just take the bag off—the clippings will either shoot all over you, or on mowers with hinged doors over the rear chute, drop in unsightly clumps. If a mulching attachment isn't available for your rear-bagging mower, a side discharge chute probably is.
- **Thatching/raking attachment.** This is one of the best ideas to come down the pike in a long time. Strong steel tines attach to the

front of the mower to pull up thatch and keep the grass straight. They will work best on self-propelled mowers with a strong vacuum action in the blade area.

- **Leaf shredders.** A heavy-duty screen installed under the deck allows you to mow up small piles of fall leaves and shred them at the same time. This makes a fantastic mulch, which can also be turned into the garden beds or composted in heaps.

OTHER LAWN MAINTENANCE EQUIPMENT

In the old days, the only way to trim around the edges after mowing was with lawn grass shears. Models with long handles were designed so you could trim without bending. Today we have gas- and electric-powered **string trimmers** to take their place.

These trimmers, often called weed whackers, spin a thick nylon filament around at high speed. The string whacks the grass off by impact. It also whacks dirt, pebbles, bark, sticks, and so forth, so **be sure to wear goggles whenever you use a string trimmer.** And to save your shins, wear long pants, too.

Ten years ago I was hesitant about buying a gas string trimmer. Their tiny engines always seemed to have problems getting going. The electric ones were very dependable, but because you had to drag a cord around, they weren't viable for commercial use. Today's small-engine technology is more advanced. With proper maintenance, these engines perform quite well. The added mobility of the gas engine makes trimming the largest of yards a breeze. Again, purchase your string trimmer at a store that will also repair it.

The string trimmer does its cutting at the end of the string. Work your way into a thick spot slowly. The more powerful the engine, the thicker the vegetation the trimmer will cut. Some models have blade attachments that allow you to cut brush and woody plants.

For a truly manicured look, a lawn should have a clean vertical edge where the grass meets the sidewalk. **Gas- and electric-powered edgers** accomplish this by spinning a flat blade vertically along the edge of the sidewalk, slicing off the grass.

Because it is much less expensive, I recommend the electric edger to most homeowners. It is not as powerful as the gas-powered, and you do have a cord to contend with, but these concerns normally will not justify the extra expense of a gas model.

Wear goggles and long pants whenever you operate a power edger. Use it when the ground is not too wet, or you'll be carving mud. Due to the design of most of the protective blade covers, you don't actually see the blade as it spins (there is usually a guide for you). The experienced landscaper learns to run the edger by ear. Keep the blade just a hair to the inside of the sidewalk and listen to the click the blade makes when it touches the sidewalk. As long as you hear an occasional click, you know the blade is not cutting too far into the lawn. Running it along the sidewalk will give you a very straight cut.

4◆WATERING THE LAWN

Water is even more important to grass plants than it is to human beings. Like people, plants are mostly water. But unlike people, grass plants have to take in almost all their nutrients dissolved in water. Without enough water in the soil, a lawn can't get the nutrients it needs for food production, growth, defense, and reproduction. It becomes a weak group of plants, easy prey for insects and disease. If there is too much water in the soil, on the other hand, the plants can drown. Again, we seek to maintain a balance.

Good soils hold water like a sponge, but allow the excess to drain off. Poorer, sandier soils barely hold water at all. Clay soils absorb water very slowly, but seem to stay wet forever once the water penetrates. These soil types are discussed thoroughly in chapter 5, *Soils*. For now it's enough to know that your soil type and the amount of rainfall you get will influence the amount of watering you must do.

SOIL MOISTURE CHANGES WITH THE WEATHER

In the springtime the ground is well saturated. As the weather grows warmer, the plants become active and start using up some of this soil moisture—those heavy bags of clippings in the spring up North are probably 90 percent water. Spring rains contain small amounts of nitrogen, a valuable plant nutrient. Give that nitrogen and water to a plant that is releasing the food it stored in its roots all winter, and you'll see the incredible growth of lawns that occurs only in the spring. Most every lawn looks lush and green at this time of year, and *additional water is not needed*.

As spring's end approaches, the soil may begin to dry out. The rain has slowed down or stopped, the sun is hotter, the air drier, and the grass roots have been steadily absorbing their dissolved nutrients. It is interesting and important to note the progression of this drying-out process. The top inch goes dry first. Within a couple weeks the top two inches may be dry. It isn't as if the entire four or six inches of topsoil dries out at the same time; it dries progressively from the top downward. A shallow-rooted lawn will wilt quickly in this situation; a deep-rooted lawn will stay green a lot longer.

An unwatered soil.

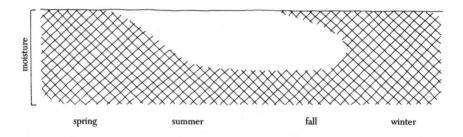

Summertime in most areas of the country means hot weather and little rain. If you don't water at all, the soil will dry out more than just a few inches down. A heavy summer rain might moisten the soil for a few days, but normally the soil will quickly dry out again. A healthy cool-season lawn will simply close up shop under these circumstances and go dormant until more favorable conditions develop. If you choose to keep the grass growing throughout the summer, you'll have to provide additional water. We'll soon discuss how to do that correctly.

Fall watering in the North is rarely a major concern, thanks to frequent rains and cooler temperatures. Most any lawn that has survived the summer will take on a rich green look again. Keeping the kids off the grass when it is soaked should concern you more at this time. A lawn takes longer to dry off in the fall, and one game of football on a saturated lawn may make a mudbath out of it. I speak from experience!

Incidentally, where I live there have been seasons in which most of September and October were completely dry. As this is a very important time in the grass plant's life—it is supposed to be growing healthily and manufacturing food for winter storage—don't put your hose away just because of the date or the temperature.

The beginning of the dry season, usually in June, is when you may remember the terrible lawn you had the past year, before you made the adjustments in mowing and fertilizing recommended by this book. You will still have that shallow-rooted, weak lawn that scarcely made it through the fall; the winter didn't magically cure it. Its lush appearance in May was just the normal spring rejuvenation, which is now ending. As the soil dries out, the shallow-rooted lawn wilts and takes on a bluish tint. When you walk on it you leave footprints because the blades don't have the strength to snap back up. The insects and disease are just licking their chops. It is a sorry state of affairs.

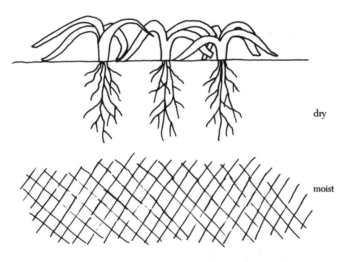

dry

moist

The obvious quick-fix for the drying out, shallow-rooted lawn is to get some water on it, fast. The lawn might die if it doesn't get some moisture, because it has used up the food it stored to take it through a dormant period. When the grass perks up and begins to grow, don't cut it until it's at least three inches tall. The leaf blade is where the plant is going to manufacture the food. Once it has some food, it will have the energy it needs to send roots deeper, reaching for the water below.

The top of the soil should nevertheless be allowed to dry out so that the roots have to reach deep for water. The roots will go deeper if the blades are high and if the top of the soil does not stay moist. A wet soil surface will encourage weed and fungus growth, and the thatchy horizontal grasses.

HOW YOUR WATERING PRACTICES AFFECT THE ROOTS

A healthy, deep-rooted lawn will go a lot longer before it shows signs of water deficiency. Remember—a healthy grass plant has a good balance of roots and topgrowth. Grass roots push quite deep into a porous soil, growing toward water as well as nutrients.

Let's suppose your lawn is healthy and fairly deep rooted. As the summer comes on the roots might look something like this:

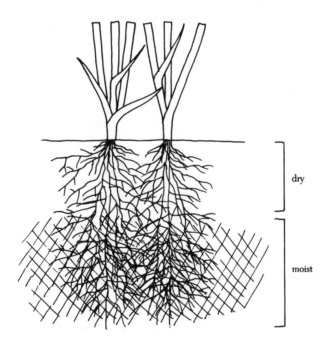

Don't water lightly at this point or you'll end up with a weak, shallow-rooted lawn. In fact, it would be better to let a healthy lawn go dormant than to water it incorrectly and make it shallow rooted. If you water each night for about twenty or thirty minutes, as many people do, the water will not penetrate deeply into the soil. Since water saturates the soil and only then moves down deeper, bit by bit, inch by inch, only the top inch or so will stay wet on a normal (not sandy) soil with this type of watering. Your grass may look like this:

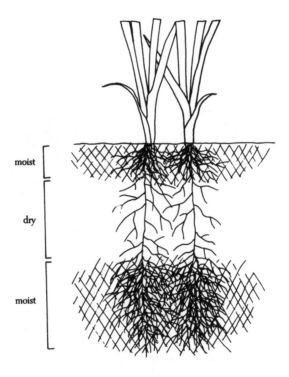

moist

dry

moist

Eventually the bottom roots die off because it is simpler for the grass to send roots just below the surface than to send them five inches down. You are left with a shallow-rooted lawn with a moist soil surface. The grass comes into stiff competition with weeds, insects, or fungus growths that thrive in the humid, jungle-like situation you have created in the midsummer heat.

WATER WISELY

Just as there is no exact formula for mowing, there is no perfect formula for watering. Sandy soils need more water; rich organic soils need less. Wind, heat, evaporation, shade, and length of grass blade

Light watering.   **Deep watering.**

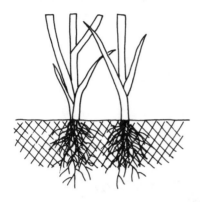
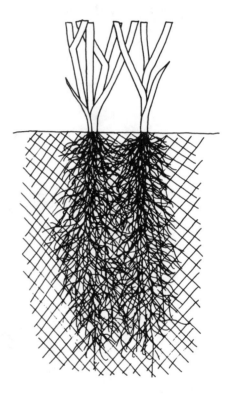

all affect your lawn's water needs. Many people with healthy lawns don't even bother to water. They allow the grass to go dormant, and it comes back to life when conditions are right.

Paul Voykin, in his book *Ask The Lawn Expert*, argues that in the cool-weather states you can hold back on watering a healthy lawn that is kept at 2½ inches or higher until late June. Then, once every seven to ten days, if there hasn't been a good rain, you should water *deeply*. I heartily agree. High grass blades will permit deeper roots, which means less watering.

A short-mowed lawn means a shallow root system and a demand for constant watering. Persistently moist soil surfaces create ideal conditions for shallow-rooted weeds (such as crabgrass), bentgrass, fungus, and various lawn diseases. On either a tall or a short lawn, too much water is trouble.

WHEN TO WATER

Begin watering your lawn when the soil has dried out well into the root zone. The higher-mown lawns should have deeper roots, so you can let them dry out more deeply between waterings.

Many factors determine how fast your soil dries out. You should encourage the roots to probe deeper by holding off on watering, but you don't want the plant to suffer from too little water. There is a fine line here. If the grass takes on a slightly bluish tint, or starts to show your footprints after you've walked over it, it is beginning to wilt. This means it is time either to water or to let the grass go dormant. If you want to, you can slice into the soil to see if the root area is moist or not.

Once you decide to water, make sure you water deeply. Water every week to ten days if you have a healthy lawn in a soil that holds water, and if there has been no substantial rain during that time. On sandy soils you might have to water twice as often.

THE TIME OF DAY TO WATER

There have always been differing opinions on the best time of day to water a lawn, but a few simple facts are all you need to know.

- Lawns need water for good health and growth.
- If the lawn surface of an unhealthy or over-chemicalized lawn stays wet for too long, it becomes susceptible to disease and insects.
- Water is precious, and shouldn't be wasted.

A lawn that is in dire need of water will benefit from it at any time—especially in the middle of ninety-degree heat. The need for water supersedes any other considerations. Don't think you mustn't water at midday because of the sunlight. The sun will not scald the grass through some sort of magnification through the water drops—that is a stubborn old fiction. If you water when it's hot and sunny you will waste some water through evaporation before it gets into the soil. On a breezy day the wind can distort the pattern of a sprinkler, blowing some water off the lawn. Water during midday heat or windy weather only if the grass needs water immediately.

Some argue that if you water at night the lawn will stay damp and invite fungus or disease. I don't think the dried-out lawn we mentioned above would have any problem with being watered at night, do you? Similarly, if we're talking about a three-inch-high lawn that hasn't seen water in a week, I don't think there's much to worry about. If you have a short-mown lawn, however, which is shallow-rooted and needs water every other day, I would definitely water it early in the day so the surface does have a chance to dry off. This is the type of lawn most lawn care books are talking about when they say you have to water in the morning or you'll get disease. That, my friends, is the type of lawn I'm trying to help you avoid. It takes much more care than the lawns this book is about.

Later on I will tell you more about handling lawn diseases naturally. At this point you should simply learn to let the top of the soil dry out thoroughly before you water. Most disease damage comes when the soil surface stays wet too long, which is why lawns in arid regions of the country rarely have disease. I turn the sprinkler on before dinner and run it until the early evening. The sun isn't very hot at that time, the wind has usually died down, and I have time to move the sprinkler around. If I didn't have to leave the house each day I would probably take extra precautions against fungus and disease by watering in the morning, to give the grass time to dry out completely by nightfall. People's jobs and other obligations often won't permit them to water at the perfect time, but that doesn't matter much to a healthy lawn. If the lawn needs moisture, water whenever it's convenient for you.

HOW MUCH WATER?

If you water deeply once every week to ten days on your three-inch-high lawn, you'll be running the sprinkler a good two to four hours, maybe more. There is no set rule. A lot depends on the sprinkler you have, your soil type, and the size of your yard. Two inches of water should be enough to penetrate any type of soil six to eight inches deep. Ideally, the water should be sprinkled on slowly enough so that it doesn't sit on top or run over the surface and into the street. You want enough water to saturate the whole topsoil layer, but you don't want to wait all day. The best way to see how far down the water has gone is to push a hand or foot spade into the lawn and tilt it forward. You should be able to observe the soil behind the spade and tell how moist it is by color or feel. After you do this a few times, you'll get to

Soil probe.

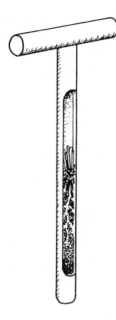

A *hollow tube pressed deep into the ground removes a core of soil. A side of the tube is missing so that you can also use this tool to observe thatch, roots, soil types, etc. Poking holes in the lawn here and there helps to aerate the lawn, as well.*

know how quickly water will penetrate your soil and you won't have to bother checking each time.

If you have a problem with water run-off, don't despair—you'll learn about the causes and corrections later. In the meantime, try a little soap and water on the lawn before each watering. Simply fill a hose-end sprayer with half water and half liquid dish soap. Spray this solution over your lawn before watering. This has several purposes: it helps break up the surface tension on the soil that keeps water from penetrating; it makes water wetter—thins it out so it can penetrate more deeply; it cleans pollutants from the grass blades; and it discourages insects and disease. Washing even a healthy lawn in this manner is a helpful practice.

Today you can purchase specialized soil soaps (called *surfactants*) and other penetrants that will "open up" the soil. Once the soil becomes healthy, such products are not needed at all.

USING A SPRINKLER

I'd like you to keep two points in mind when you use a sprinkler. First, make sure you water deeply enough. Second, make sure to distribute the water uniformly across the lawn.

Pouring a gallon of water over one square foot of your lawn will saturate that spot quickly. But when you distribute a gallon of water over 1000 square feet—as a sprinkler might—you haven't done much for the lawn. Depending on your sprinkler and water pressure, it could take hours to distribute one inch of water. What really counts is not applying a certain number of inches or gallons, but making sure you run the sprinkler until the water penetrates down through the dry soil and into the moist area. Remember, water moves through the soil little by little. The best way to tell if the ground has been thoroughly watered is to use a soil probe or to push a spade into the ground.

WHICH SPRINKLER IS RIGHT FOR YOU?

There are probably more than a dozen sprinkler styles: in-ground, oscillating, rotating, fan style, travelling, and impulse, to name a few. No matter which type you use, you must make sure the water is evenly distributed over your lawn, or you'll end up with areas that are too wet or too dry. The only practical way for a homeowner to test his sprinkler's water distribution is to set up cans or buckets to catch the water at various distances from the sprinkler. Run this test at the time you would normally water the lawn so that water pressure doesn't become a variable.

Once you know how your sprinkler actually distributes water, you can move the sprinkler around as needed to ensure that the whole lawn gets an equal share of water.

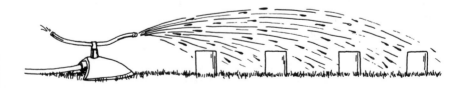

Space cans or buckets evenly to one side of the sprinkler.

REGIONAL DIFFERENCES

The top 6–8 inches of your soil should stay moist in order to support a conventional lawn. For most of the eastern U.S. and upper Pacific Coast regions, this occurs with minimal watering to supplement normal rainfall. Of course, local conditions, such as heat, soil type, and wind can make a difference. The areas between the Great Plains and the Pacific mountain ranges, and much of California, have mostly arid or semi-arid conditions. Don't expect to be able to grow a fine lawn in these regions without applying 4–5 inches of water per month. The prohibitive cost of water leads many people in these regions to be satisfied with tougher, paler native grasses that don't have high water demands. (See map on page 83, *Grass Types by Region*.)

Before moving on to the next section, keep in mind these few tips.

- **Each part of your yard is different.** The higher areas will generally drain faster and therefore need more water. The lower areas will need less water, and might even collect some run-off from rains or watering.
- **Rains can be deceptive.** A shower or downpour can add less water to your lawn than you might think. Check carefully before deciding that rain took the place of a watering. You might even want to water right after a rain if it wasn't quite enough.
- **Stay off the grass directly after watering or after a rainfall.** You don't want to make foot impressions in the soil, or tear up the grass and create a mudbath.
- **Shaded areas need less watering.**
- **If there are trees on the lawn, be careful to water more heavily right under them.** Trees consume enormous amounts of water. Make sure to water deeply, and keep the surface dry or you'll encourage tree roots in the grass.

5♦THE SOIL

The basic building block of a healthy lawn is a healthy soil. Remember this principle! If you try to understand natural lawn care without knowing anything about soil, you're going to miss the boat. Aside from air and sunlight, almost everything else a plant needs enters it by way of the roots. Your cutting, watering, and fertilizing practices will all affect the quality of your soil.

There are good soils and bad soils, and soil can get better or worse. Fortunately for us, the subject of soil needs to be understood only at a very basic level.

WHAT MAKES A SOIL GOOD?

Good or bad soil isn't just a question of fertility. A soil could be loaded with nutrients and still be unable to produce a healthy plant. **Soil texture**, **soil structure**, and **soil life** determine whether soil is good or bad. A good soil allows air, water, nutrients, and roots to move through it easily. It holds water like a sponge, yet permits excess water to drain away before the grass drowns. It is alive with microorganisms, worms, and other beneficial life forms which work constantly on minerals (rocks) and decaying matter, breaking them down into solutions that are usable for plant nutrition. This is what the soils of the midwestern plains were like when the settlers arrived. And this is the direction in which you should be heading as you learn how to build up your own soil.

TOPSOIL

The *American Heritage Dictionary* defines soil as "the top layer of the earth's surface, suitable for the growth of plant life." Just how suitable your soil may be is the question. If you were to take a side view of the soil under your lawn, you would probably see two distinct layers. Above is the *topsoil*, usually somewhat loose and dark; under that is the *subsoil*, often hard and clay-like, or coarse and sandy.

The depth of your topsoil depends on what was done before your lawn was put in. If your house was built on a field or in woodlands, and the contractor didn't strip the topsoil off, you might have four or eight inches or more of good topsoil—lucky you! Typically, however, the builder pushes the topsoil to the side for other uses. When the house is completed he'll grade the subsoil smooth (and hard) and then put a couple inches of topsoil back on. That's just enough for grass seed or sod to take root in. The rest of the topsoil might be sold or used to make planting beds. Sometimes a contractor will bring in fresh topsoil that turns out to be more like shredded subsoil. When it

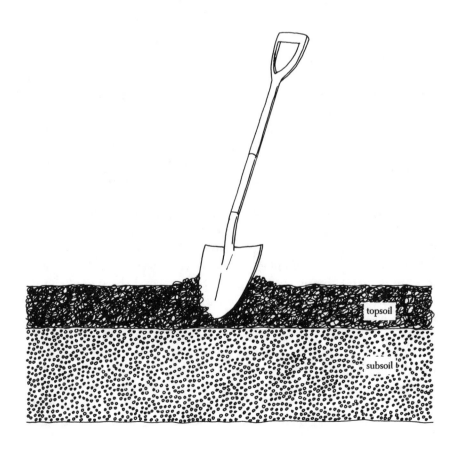

soaks up a little moisture it turns into a hard-crusted, cracked sheet. Grass can grow in this, but weeds do better. Consider yourself lucky if your builder hired a competent landscaper to supply enough topsoil for a healthy lawn to grow in.

You really should dig into your soil and see where the shovel hits the subsoil. If you have at least 5–6 inches of topsoil under the lawn, you're in good shape. If not, you could pull up the lawn and add more, but that's not a job most of us are interested in doing. With some patience, you can rehabilitate the soil you have, and at the same time transform some of the subsoil into real topsoil. The process begins with an understanding of what soil is and how it is formed.

SOIL vs. DIRT

Soil is not dirt. Don't interchange the two words unless you want to insult a lot of conscientious gardeners. Use the word dirt to describe the stuff you find behind the kitchen stove, or for earth that has very little ability to support plant life. Real soil must contain water, air, minerals (rock particles), and most important, **organic matter,** or **humus.** By organic matter I mean anything once living (plant life, bacteria, worms, insects) but now decayed or in the process of decaying. In the advanced stages of decay, organic matter becomes distinctly different from what it originally was. It becomes a dark, crumbly, fine-textured and extremely valuable substance called humus. Take the humus out of a soil, and then you can call it dirt.

The more humus, the better the soil structure will be. Humus is full of beneficial organisms. It is sponge-like in its water-holding capabilities. Its presence helps make the soil more porous and fertile. The major differences between your topsoil and the subsoil beneath it is the amount of humus it contains, and the size of the rock particles in it. A good topsoil will have 3–10 percent humus. A subsoil might have 1 percent or less. The deeper you go down, the less humus and soil life you will find. If you want to turn your subsoil into real soil, you're going to have to find a way to get more humus and soil life into it. Nowadays you can buy bagged humus at many garden centers, and this is a great step forward for natural gardening. But you shouldn't rely on storebought humus. Use the information in this book and create your own humus and soil life right under your lawn.

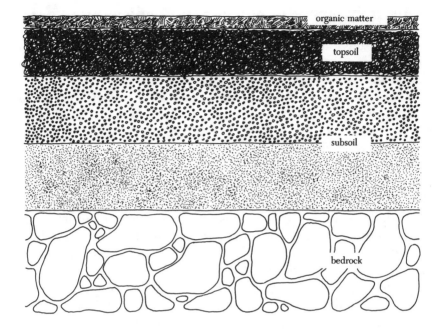

HOW SOIL WAS FORMED

The formation of soil from pure rock, which the earth used to be, took millions of years, and happened as a result of both physical stress (wind, rain, heat, cold, expansion, contraction) and biological activity. The first biological activity on the rock was only the slow attack of single-celled microbes. When these microbes died, their bodies (which were organic matter) mixed with tiny fragments of rock, as well as water and air, and formed the first soil. This soil, though extremely thin, could support higher life forms, such as fungi and lichens. Eventually mosses developed which had penetrating root hairs that helped speed the decomposition of rock. As a result of this constant activity, a shallow layer of soil began to build up. The plant life that grew in this thin soil hastened the soil formation process. These plants were able to send out stronger roots to dig deeper, and they dropped plenty of organic matter (leaves and stems) on the ground to feed worms and other soil life. But even after many millions of years, nature has provided us with precious little topsoil. It is not all right for us to deplete this topsoil or to let it erode.

SOIL TEXTURE: CLAY SOILS, SANDY SOILS, AND LOAMS

Not all soils turned out the same. Depending on what the original rock was, and the physical and biological factors affecting it, a topsoil can be any one of hundreds of types.

When rock breaks down, it turns into sand particles (small), silt particles (barely visible), or clay particles (microscopic). Sand and silt are very similar except in size, so they are often grouped together as "sand." Clay particles are so tiny that they are somewhat chemically active, and thus they bond together. They can hold and be converted into nutrients. Organic matter and soil life are powerful natural forces that work to separate clay and allow air and water to penetrate. They also help to bond the clay's various-sized particles together into rough-shaped granules, which form the structure we know as soil. Without the organic matter and soil life, there would just be a layer of rock particles, which I call dirt.

The ideal soil is called **loam**. A loam is simply a soil that contains a mixture of sand, silt, and clay particles, as well as organic matter. If the particles in your soil are anywhere from 10–25 percent clay, the balance being sand and silt, you have a good loam. A sandy loam has slightly less clay, but at least 5 percent of it. Any less clay than that in a soil pretty much makes it sand. A clay loam is between 25 and 35 percent clay. Any more than that you would simply call clay, and start making pottery instead of a lawn.

Here is a very simple way to determine the make-up of your soil:

1. Get a large glass jar with a lid.
2. Put in a small amount of your topsoil (about two inches).
3. Add water, about 4–5 times the amount of the soil.
4. Shake vigorously for two minutes.
5. Allow to settle overnight.

The sand particles, being larger and heavier, will settle to the bottom first. Then comes the silt layer. The clay will sit on top of that layer. On top of the clay will be a thin layer of organic and living matter. The water will be filled with murky soil life, and you might find some larger pieces of organic matter floating on top. Note how thin the layer of organic matter is. Don't fail to recognize the importance of this!

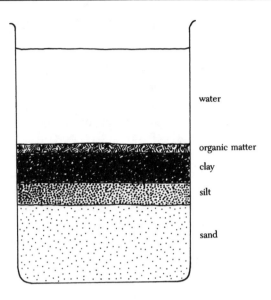

water

organic matter

clay

silt

sand

Try this test on different sections of your lawn and flower beds, and note the differences. You may be quite surprised by the results, and you'll get a closer understanding of just what is in your soil. For instance, in my town the topsoil is heavy clay. You never see sand particles in it. Yet when I did this simple soil test in my yard, I found that my own soil was actually about 70 percent sand. I had a pretty good clay loam, better than I had thought.

A good loam absorbs rain quickly and holds it, while letting the excess drain off. It is usually slightly damp, and will hold together in a ball if you squeeze it in your hand, but will separate and crumble easily. I like to compare it to the feel of a handful of raisins squeezed together, then broken apart with a quick rub of your fingers.

A sandy soil, without enough humus in it, will dry out too fast. It feels gritty to the touch. Clay soil absorbs water slowly and dries out slowly, because it lacks space between its particles. It will feel rubbery when wet. Working a wet clay soil or clay loam is a big mistake. You will break down the soil's structure, causing a rock-hard, bonded soil when it dries. You can add sand to a clay soil, and vice versa, but that doesn't help too much. To make a permanent change, one that leads to better structure, texture, and greater fertility, you must add organic matter, and lots of it. Organic matter will bring both sandy and clay soils closer to the ideal.

THE IMPORTANCE OF SOIL STRUCTURE

The term **soil structure** refers to the way individual particles in the soil group themselves together into **granules**—small centers of activity that hold onto moisture and nutrients. The space that exists between granules allows for air penetration and water drainage. Very sandy soils show little granulation. Clay soils tend to granulate more, but this granulation is quickly destroyed if the soil is worked when wet, or if the soil becomes compacted.

The topsoil formation process I spoke of earlier is still going on today. The subsoil is barely soil, but it isn't rock anymore, either. The combined effects of soil life, organic matter, weather activity, and other influences create more topsoil. Unfortunately, there are also conditions today that kill off the life in some soils, on both lawns and farms. The soil in many places is actually getting worse. The reason for this is twofold. First, there is soil depletion, which is mostly a farming problem but which also occurs in lawns. The soil's nutrients and organic matter are used up by cultivated plants and not replaced. The plants themselves (or their clippings) are removed and not re-cycled into the soil, and eventually the soil becomes so depleted that its structure breaks down.

The second reason for the worsening of soils is improper or exces-sive use of chemicals. Many of today's lawn and farm chemicals chase away and kill off soil life, as well as break down soil structure. The chemical fertilizers release too quickly to be absorbed by the plants. A soil inundated with agricultural or lawn chemicals can lose the valu-able bonding materials created by the soil microbes. In very small doses most of these chemicals are not too harmful, especially if there is already enough humus in the soil to buffer the chemicals' effects. But when applied too heavily, these chemicals become poisonous to the health of any soil. Humans, in their infinite wisdom, have actually figured out how to unmake soil. The sad part is that few realize that this is going on today wherever strong chemicals are overused.

One very simple way of immediately helping to improve your soil structure is through the use of a soil conditioner. This will temporarily improve structure while you work at building up a healthy soil. Soil conditioner will help break up the heavier, compacted soils as well as help aggregate the sandier soils and improve their moisture-holding capabilities. The better organic soil conditioners also add soil nutrients that unlock soil elements and help speed up the formation of a good living soil from a poor one. Once your soil has become full of life and has the proper structure, it can be easily maintained with basic natural lawn care practices.

It should be evident by now that a living soil will lead to good soil structure. Starting out with a loam instead of a clay or sandy soil would make this goal much easier to achieve, but many of you don't have a loam and are going to have to work at building one. I'm going to summarize the importance of good soil structure by paraphrasing a fact sheet given to me by Dr. Herbert C. Dostal of Four Star Agricultural Services. Here are the benefits of good soil structure:

- Improved soil aeration. Water drains quickly and doesn't sit in the root zone; therefore roots develop strongly and quickly, soil life flourishes, and the likelihood of soil-borne diseases diminishes.
- Good structure means less compaction from foot traffic because the soil doesn't stay wet.
- Soil warms up quicker, seeds sprout faster, and plants grow faster.
- No dry spots. With good structure, water is held.
- Improved nitrogen release because soil microbes can work on decaying matter. Also, nitrogen doesn't drain away.
- Better weed control. Many weeds only sprout in very wet or very dry soil. And the superior lawn that a good soil structure produces will crowd out weeds, too.
- Less erosion. Water penetrates and soil doesn't wash away because the granules are bonded together.

And I'll add:

- Increased fertility. A living soil converts minerals and organic matter into nutrients safely and almost endlessly.

The solution to almost any soil problem is the addition of organic matter, which will soon convert to humus. Simplistic as it may sound, the way to a better soil is to create a better soil. The chapter on fertilizing will tell you what to add to your soil to turn it into the ideal growing medium for grass. With a good soil, plus proper mowing and watering, your lawn problems will be few.

6 ◆ FERTILIZING

Is it really necessary to fertilize lawns? For most homeowners, the answer is yes. But if you have a well-structured soil, full of worms and other soil life, and you can leave most of your clippings to decompose, then your fertilizer needs will be minimal. Think of fertilizing as soil building instead of plant feeding. Natural fertilizers will increase soil life, improve structure, and provide nutrients. The minerals and nutrients in a living soil are quickly broken down and made available for the roots to take in. In fact, a living soil can manufacture certain nutrients from the atmosphere as well as from soil matter. This doesn't take place in a soil that has had the life in it killed off, which is one reason why established, living soils need significantly less fertilizer. A living soil is capable of producing a large part of a lawn's fertilizer needs on its own, especially if the clippings are recycled.

THE SYNTHETIC AND THE NATURAL

Let's take a good look at the differences between synthetic chemical and natural fertilizers. Natural fertilizers come from plant and animal sources, or from rock powders. These include bone meal, dehydrated manures, cottonseed meal, seaweed and fish products, and granite dust. There are currently scores of natural products available in pure and combined forms. Such materials break down slowly to provide long-term nutrition and steady rather than excessive growth. They also encourage soil life and help build better soil structure. Certain beneficial bacteria, aided by natural fertilizers, absorb nitrogen from the atmosphere and fix it (release it) into the soil. Other bacteria form hormones which stimulate root growth. A few of the better natural fertilizer blends contain additional beneficial bacteria and enzymes so the soil will come back to life more quickly. These superior fertilizers often provide **trace elements,** vital nutrients that plants need in minute quantities. It is almost impossible to harm a lawn with natural fertilizers.

Natural fertilizers have very few drawbacks. True, they usually take a while to break down, especially when first introduced on a cold, dead, or half-dead soil, but quick-fix, instant results are not nature's way. Gradual yet lasting changes benefit the lawn more in the long run. Some natural fertilizers have an odor, but the odor is not long-lasting, especially when the fertilizer is put on a living soil that quickly breaks it down into usable nutrients. Most brands are deodorized now, and watering after fertilizing will help speed things up. You'll find natural fertilizers bulkier than chemical fertilizers, and the bulk does enable more uniform application. Though sometimes more expensive than chemical fertilizers, I have found natural fertilizers to be ultimately quite economical.

Synthetic chemical fertilizers act quickly, if that is what you want. They can make a bad lawn look better faster than most natural fertilizers can. Their ingredient proportions are precise, so that you can easily compute exactly how much of each nutrient your lawn is getting (though how much your lawn actually needs is still a guess). And they are often inexpensive.

Here are the drawbacks of chemical fertilizers. They release their nutrients *too* quickly, creating excessive topgrowth before the roots can catch up. Not only does this kind of growth weaken the grass, but you may find yourself struggling to cut a six-inch-high lawn two days after the spraying company fertilized.

Much of a quickly released fertilizer tends to get leached away, especially on sandy soils. **If you use chemical fertilizers, try them in small quantities applied frequently.** This will prevent over-fertilizing, prevent waste from leaching, and allow the soil to buffer harmful effects much more easily. Most chemical fertilizers can burn a lawn if it's not watered soon. Their high salt concentration literally sucks moisture from the grass plants.

An overabundance of chemicals in the soil will chase away earthworms, and that is a gardening crime. Let me digress here a bit. Earthworms ingest soil and decaying plant material and leave behind **castings** (up to 40 pounds per 1000 square feet in a healthy soil). These castings are extremely rich in nutrients, and in fact are actually collected by some people and sold to florists as fertilizer and soil conditioner. This fertilizer is an additional benefit that you get from natural gardening methods, and for you it's free. Earthworms can burrow into the harder subsoil. Their castings enhance microbial activity down deep, which helps turn subsoil into topsoil. Some species of worms burrow right up to the top of the soil and chew up grass clippings. While they are on top, they leave castings which aid decomposition. These castings are unsightly only on fancy, short-cropped lawns. On regular lawns you don't see them. For most homeowners, the more earthworms the better.

Let me quote Paul Voykin from his book *Ask the Lawn Expert* on his experience with earthworms. "A long time ago I noticed this significant natural phenomenon: Whenever lawns, gardens, or golf courses had an abundant earthworm population, the turf had a strong root system and much less thatch, and was healthy-looking even when undernourished. . . . Believe me, no machine can duplicate the natural aerification process caused by Mother Nature's snaky little creatures."

Chemical lawn fertilizer is also capable of killing off many of the soil microbes that are responsible for decomposition, soil formation, nutrient production, and protection from fungus and other lawn diseases. Stronger chemicals ruin soil structure by dissolving the bonding materials (formed by microbes) that hold soil particles together, and can turn topsoil into the cementlike crust you may have noticed in the pots of houseplants that are regularly fed typical plant food. Many chemical fertilizers contain acids which in turn make the soil acid. The liquid forms, especially, encourage shallow rooting and thatch formation.

Chemical fertilizers will improve a poor soil by adding nutrients to it, but when misapplied, or applied for the wrong reason, they can ruin the structure and life of even the best soils. After a while, an over-chemicalized lawn gets no nutrition at all from the soil. It becomes totally dependent on synthetic nutrients—and on your willingness to purchase and apply them regularly.

ENVIRONMENTAL INFLUENCES

Most people are quite aware of the possible toxic effects of synthetic pesticides and herbicides. But if you were to ask them if there is anything wrong with synthetic *fertilizers*, they couldn't really answer that one. So I'll give you a quick summary.

First of all, as mentioned previously, synthetic chemical fertilizers, if misused, will kill off soil life, and will ruin the soil structure if there isn't enough humus available to buffer their effects.

Additionally, chemical lawn fertilizers are similar to agricultural fertilizers in the way they can affect the water supply. The quick-release nitrogen leaches through a porous soil very fast—perhaps only half of it gets used by the grass, and the excess nitrogen seeps into the groundwater and ends up in streams and ponds. This causes algae build-up, reduction of the water's oxygen, and eventually a dead body of water. Excessive nitrogen (or nitrates, to be exact) and the chemical compounds it breaks down into, have been shown to be toxic to man and beast. This is no longer just a concern about farming practices. With all the chemical lawn fertilizers being applied by both home-owners and commercial outfits today, the possibility of this type of pollution affecting you and me is very real.

Some chemical fertilizers are called slow-release, or synthetic-organic. They behave something like natural fertilizers in that they don't instantly release into the soil. Other chemical fertilizers contain fast-release and slow-release chemicals (usually nitrogen). You can usually tell if a fertilizer has slow-release nitrogen because the label will specify W.I.N.—water-insoluble nitrogen. W.I.N. may also refer to the *organic* nitrogen content of a fertilizer if there are some organic components in the bag. If you can't get all natural fertilizer, this is next best. If only quick-release chemicals are available, go ahead and buy them. Just remember to apply them gradually in small amounts. In the meantime, continue your search for organic fertilizers, and consult the list of suppliers in the back of this book. For with too much chemical use, your soil will become quite dead.

Your lawn's ability to withstand the attendant problems of chemicals depends upon the amount of humus in the soil and the amount (and types) of chemicals you apply. Once the balance starts to favor the chemicals, it won't be long before you have your very own toxic waste dump—or at least thatch and other dead soil problems.

Before I end this comparison there is one other point I should mention. Many agronomists say that there are no real differences between natural and synthetic fertilizers as they enter the roots of plants. I don't believe this, and many people agree with me. True, the basic chemical structure might be the same, but this is only the structure that we know how to look at with current technology. There may be multitudes of intrinsic differences yet to be found. It should also be remembered that the nutrients in natural fertilizers are com-bined with other beneficial substances. These naturally occurring combinations will contribute subtle influences that a straight synthetic nutrient will lack.

Living things contain life-force, theta, or whatever you choose to call it. It isn't animated—it does the animating. It is not something that a microscope can find, but it is there. I have seen specialized photos, using a process called chromatography, of natural and synthetic vitamins, and curiously enough the natural ones have a radiant glow, while the synthetic ones appear flat. Scientists can't explain this phenomenon well, but I believe it is just a manifestation of the life that is there. I'm positive it is the same story with fertilizers. Putting life into living things seems a lot saner to me than putting synthetics into living things.

ACID OR ALKALINE?

I mentioned earlier that chemical fertilizers make soils more acid. This brings up a subject you should know something about. Aside from classifying soils as sandy or clay, we also classify them as acid or alkaline. Scientists measure just how acid or alkaline a soil is by measuring its pH. If you enjoy chemistry, look up what pH means literally. Otherwise, the pH scale below is simple enough to understand and use.

	ACID			NEUTRAL			ALKALINE			
<———————————————							—————————————————>			
0 1 2 3 4 5 6 7 8 9 10 11 12 13 14										

When a soil is tested for pH, the test will result in a number. Seven is exactly neutral, so anything below that is acid to some degree, and anything above is alkaline. Most lawn grasses seem to do best between 7.5 and 6; that is, generally neutral or slightly acid. Keeping the pH in the right range is extremely important. If the soil is too acid or alkaline, the nutrients in the soil will become unavailable. When you seem to be doing everything right for your lawn but it isn't responding, the soil's pH might be off.

The pH of a soil is mostly determined by the type of rock the soil developed from, and the amount of humus in the soil. The presence of lawn grasses will tend to make a soil more acid over time due to certain gases the grass releases through respiration. It shouldn't surprise you that in the same pH that lawns grow best, soil microbes are the most active. Too acid or too alkaline means death to the majority of the beneficial soil life forms. Imbalances of pH also cause a dissolving of a soil's bonding particles, and a breakdown of its structure.

Often, just by adding organic matter and natural fertilizers to a soil, you can bring a soil closer to a neutral pH. Organic matter will release weak acids upon decomposition, so its use in an alkaline soil will bring the pH down. But in general, organic matter will moderate either a very acid or very alkaline soil.

If your lawn isn't doing fine already, have your soil tested for pH. At best, a test will tell you that your soil is fine, and at worst it will tell you that it has a pH imbalance you were not aware of. A good nursery person will know what type of soil is common in your area, but should perhaps test the pH for you to make sure. If your soil was trucked in, it might be completely different from the rest of your neighborhood's.

Every part of the United States has a Cooperative Extension Service which will help you get your soil tested, and almost every state has a Land Grant College that tests soil as part of its responsibilities to the state. If you want to do the testing yourself, you can buy an inexpensive pH test kit or pH meter at a garden center.

IF YOUR SOIL IS ACID

Continue to add organic matter and natural fertilizers no matter what your soil's pH is. If it's on the acid side, add ground limestone, available at any garden center. Use dolomite limestone if it's available, because, except on heavy clay soils that are high in magnesium, it provides a necessary nutrient (magnesium). Lime takes a while to alkalize (raise the pH of) a soil, so don't expect drastic changes the first season you apply it.

Also keep in mind that lime is a good soil conditioner for acid soils. Ground limestone on a clay soil will tend to separate the clay particles by causing them to group up, and it will do the same for sandy soils. This is highly desirable, because grouped particles result in less overall space in the soil, and therefore greater water and nutrient retention.

Of course, the agricultural chemical companies have developed

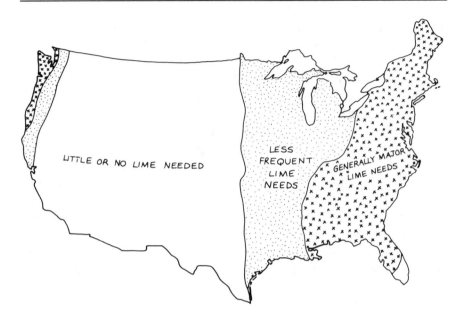

something called "quicklime." Yes, it does work faster to raise the pH, but it can kill off a soil's life and reduce its fertility. Again, it's too much at once for the soil to use correctly. Avoid it. "Hydrated lime" is also commonly found in garden shops these days. It isn't as harmful as quicklime, but it should be used at half to two-thirds the amount of ground limestone (or follow package directions). If plain ground limestone is available, use that and let nature handle the rest.

Lime should be applied with a fertilizer spreader—never with your bare hands, because it can burn. The amount of lime to use depends on the type of soil you have and the degree to which you want to raise the pH. On a good loam, 70 pounds of ground limestone for every 1000 square feet of lawn surface will raise the pH one full number. On a sandy soil, 40–50 pounds will raise it the same amount; very sandy soil will need even less. A heavy clay soil requires 80–90 pounds per 1000 square feet to raise the pH by a factor of one.

Some experts feel that you shouldn't apply more than 75 pounds of lime per 1000 square feet in one season because it can lock up other soil minerals. So if your soil is going to need a lot of lime, it might be better to divide the applications over two seasons. Early spring or fall liming (but never in contact with new grass seed) will give the best results.

Pure powdered sulfur can be used for lowering the pH of an alkaline soil. The recommended rate is one pound per 100 square feet to lower the pH one full point. You can apply powdered sulfur at half this rate and do a spring and fall application. Apply it only after an accurate soil test.

Other natural alkalizing substances include wood ashes, ground marble, ground oyster shells, and bone meal. If wood ashes from a fireplace are readily available, sift out the coals and spread the ashes at about two-thirds the rate for lime, or five gallons per 1000 square feet. You might have to broadcast the ashes by hand (wearing gloves)—just be careful that they don't get heavy in any one spot. Marble, oyster shells, and bone meal are rarely used as alkalizers on a lawn, probably due to cost as much as anything else. Bone meal usually comes packaged alone or in natural fertilizer blends, but is generally used for its great fertilizing value rather than its slight alkalizing effect.

IF YOU HAVE ALKALINE SOIL

What about alkaline soil that needs to have its pH lowered? Of course, the addition of organic matter will help, but when it has to be applied on top of a lawn it must be finely ground. Cottonseed meal is a good acidifier as well as fertilizer, and I use it on all my evergreens. It is found packaged in the better garden centers. Gypsum (calcium sulfate) is even more common, and less expensive. It is a naturally occurring chemical compound (and the major component of plaster). Because it is found in a compound state, some purists argue that it isn't strictly a natural product. But it is commonly used because it is seemingly benign and is an excellent soil conditioner. If availability and economics lead you to use it, continue to add organic matter until the pH is under control. Gypsum will help soak up any chemicals that can get on the lawn, such as dog urine, gas, oil, and salt from snow removal equipment. Just sprinkle it over any affected spot. Wait until the end of the winter to treat road salts.

Most of the chemical products used to lower pH and make soils more acid contain sulphur. Sulphur products should always be used very carefully, and only after a soil test recommended rate is determined. It's easy to overdo it. The use of straight powdered sulphur is not recommended because it has adverse affects on soil life. In fact, sulphur is used frequently as a fungicide. There is another sulphur we get for free: it comes from the smokestacks of the industrial plants and falls to earth in the form of acid rain. People who get a lot of acid rain must keep up with their alkalizing program.

If you fertilize naturally and follow sound gardening practices, your soil will continue to improve year after year. If you get its pH tested and brought into the proper range, the improvement will be that much faster. The right pH means more soil life, and all the benefits which that life provides for the health of the grass and the condition of the soil.

NATURAL FERTILIZERS

What exactly should you put on your lawn to fertilize it? How important are those numbers on the sides of fertilizer bags? Do you need a degree in chemistry and math to understand what you are doing?

Don't worry—natural lawn fertilizing is simple. The numbers on the fertilizer bags have nominal importance to you because you are interested in fertilizer more as a soil builder than as a direct plant feeder. You are trying to create and maintain a living, healthy soil that will provide an ideal environment for the grass plant. If you depended on chemicals, you wouldn't expect the soil to provide anything but a root base for the grass plant, so those numbers on the fertilizer bag really would matter. They would represent the only significant nutrition your lawn would ever get, especially if it was chemical-dependent and consequently growing in dead soil.

THREE MAJOR NUTRIENTS

Nobody knows exactly what a plant's needs are, but the majority of these needs have been isolated. We know that natural fertilizers provide, in their complexity, a broader spectrum of nutrients than the more exactly proportioned chemical fertilizers.

The three major nutrients plants use are nitrogen (N), phosphorus (P), and potassium (K). Each has specific value to a grass plant.

Nitrogen (N) not only feeds grass, but helps sustain soil life. It is necessary for healthy aboveground growth and green color. Without it, lawns are stunted and yellowish. With too much at once, the grass grows too fast for its own good, resulting in weak, disease-prone blades. Most organic materials release nitrogen as they decompose; this is considered **slow-release** nitrogen. **Quick-release** nitrogen enters the soil as soon as the fertilizer becomes moist. Because nitrogen can be washed away with water, it is very important to have a continuous supply being made.

Phosphorus (P) encourages strong and quick root growth, and helps plants resist disease. A phosphorus deficiency shows up in poor rooting, slow growth and an off-color—yellow, or perhaps a purple tint. Most soils contain sufficient phosphorous, but only a living soil can release it.

Potassium (K), usually called **potash**, assists in the production and movement of food throughout a plant, improves the hardiness of plant tissue, builds resistance to disease, and protects from heat and cold. It is formed during decomposition of organic matter, and can be leached away by water. Many soils contain potash in mineral form, which can then slowly be made available to plants as the soil life acts on it.

A continuous supply of N, P, and K, the primary plant nutrients, will mean a better lawn. Iron is one of the minor nutrients, or **trace elements**, that can be applied; it can have a visible effect within twenty-four hours. Lack of iron causes chlorosis, a yellowing of new leaves. Many gardeners, seeing yellow blades, assume there is a nitrogen deficiency. But if additional nitrogen doesn't cure it, iron usually will. Supplemental iron makes grass green without forcing it to grow taller.

But there are ten other known elements that grass needs in lesser quantities. Calcium, magnesium, and sulfur are considered the secondary nutrients. Iron, manganese, copper, boron, zinc, chlorine, and molybdenum are called **minor nutrients**. Many soils contain a good supply of these elements, but without proper pH and enough soil life, they become unavailable. Most natural fertilizers contain some of these nutrients. Others, especially sea products, contain many valuable trace elements—helpful substances that, though not entirely vital, will enhance plant growth in one or more ways.

All nutrients have importance, but don't get hung up looking for problems you don't have. Farmers have done well for centuries without even knowing their names. Amish farmers, for example, still follow their old methods, using crop rotation, animal manure, and green manures (inexpensive, specialized crops that are turned back into the soil to add structure and fertility), and they grow consistently high quality products. F.H. King, in *Farmers of Forty Centuries*, shows how Chinese farmers grow as many as five crops a year in the same plot, without the benefit of chemicals or any knowledge of N, P, and K. They make their soil rich and productive by taking all the organic matter they can find—plant residues, leaves, sawdust, rice hulls, animal manure, human waste (they call it "night soil")—and putting it back into the land. The Chinese compost organic materials by methods handed down from generation to generation, piling organic matter into layered heaps that heat up enough to kill off unhealthy bacteria. It then quickly decomposes to form the richest humus one could imagine.

I realize that for many homeowners composting seems impractical or just too much trouble. The point I'm trying to make is that traditional farmers get good results solely by natural methods, with no concern for N, P, or K. The result is a fertile, living, healthy soil that plants thrive in.

The chemical companies recommend that you fertilize by applying a specified number of pounds of each nutrient per 1000 square feet. Their researchers have determined how much of each of these ingredients a plant uses every year, and advise you to apply that much when you fertilize. To help you with this, most fertilizer bags have numbers on them like 5-10-5, 6-2-2, and so on. These numbers represent percentages of N, P, and K, always in that order. For example, the number 4-2-3 on a fifty-pound bag of fertilizer means that 4 percent of the weight of the ingredients is nitrogen, 2 percent is phosphorus, and 3 percent is potash. This works out to be 2 pounds of nitrogen, 1 pound of phosphorus, and 1½ pounds of potash. In a bag of chemical fertilizer, the remainder of the weight is filler, perhaps ground chalk which will neutralize some of the acidifying effects of the chemical fertilizer. Sometimes a concentrated liquid fertilizer is sprayed right onto a carrier in concentrated form. This accounts for the way some chemical fertilizers are able to cover large areas with very small and light packages. The surplus weight in a bag of organic fertilizer is most likely fiber, or something else that will improve the soil.

What the synthetic lawn chemical manufacturers don't take into account is the amount of nutrients that can be created or recycled in a naturally cared-for lawn. I've already mentioned the ability of certain bacteria to capture atmospheric nitrogen, and the nutrients that become available as the soil life works on minerals and organic matter. Probably the best sources of plant nutrition are dead and decaying grass roots, and especially grass clippings decomposing into the soil. They provide a 4-1-3 fertilizer, which is about as perfect a combination as any lawn needs.

Clippings alone provide about two pounds of nitrogen per 1000 square feet of lawn a year. With the continued recycling of roots and clippings, plus proper mowing and watering, and maybe a little lime every few years, you can have a thriving lawn. Fertilizer needs will be minimal because almost every nutrient is being recycled.

The chemical fertilizer people don't take any of this into account when they say that you and your neighbors need to apply their Super Duper Grass Builder 20-5-5 four times a year, every year, to maintain a nice-looking lawn. They do not mention thatch and other problems a steady diet high in chemical fertilizers can create. Eliot Roberts, Director of The Lawn Institute, has this to say about these high chemical recommendations:

> The turf does look better, and for the professional grounds manager who can use insecticides, fungicides, and herbicides to keep the grass going, it is more suitable for golf and sports activities. *But it's not healthy.* (My emphasis added.) This is where the home gardener gets into trouble, because turf superintendents get into trouble too, at times.

In terms of N-P-K, lawns generally like a 4-1-2 fertilizer. *This does not have to be exact!* Natural fertilizers may provide a 6-1-1, 2-1-1, 5-2-3, or any similar formula and still bring good results. Most garden centers do not carry balanced natural fertilizers that are designed primarily for lawn use, though this will change if you and I encourage them to carry some of the natural products that are available. I would support any endeavor to get natural products marketed broadly, and I hope you will, too. Until you can purchase a complete lawn fertilizer, you might have to mix together some of the natural products that are easily available.

SOIL TESTS

The majority of you won't bother with this, and that's fine, but the best way to determine the condition of your soil is to have a complete soil test done. Your Cooperative Extension agent can provide this service or tell you who will. It will determine pH, plus the major nutrients your soil needs. Some tests will also tell you the humus content of your soil. Get a diagnosis, but decide for yourself how to apply it to your lawn.

More than likely, you will be advised to use chemical solutions for soil deficiencies. Forget it. A good nursery will carry enough natural fertilizers to render chemicals unnecessary. It's time to start building a healthy soil and lawn, if you are not doing so already. It can only be done naturally!

If you don't get a complete soil test, just try to add a decent balance of nutrients to your lawn. I found the following natural fertilizers at my local nursery:

NATURAL FERTILIZERS

Product	N	P	K
Deodorized fish fertilizer (liquid)	5	1	1
Dehydrated manure (mixed)	3	2	2
Dehydrated cow manure	2	1	2
Bone meal (steamed)	1	23	0
Cottonseed meal	6	1	1
Dried blood	10	1	0
Milorganite (granulated sewage sludge)	6	3	0
All & Only (blend)	5	5	5

The All & Only and dried blood were, unfortunately, available only in five-pound bags, and would be quite costly used as the sole fertilizer. The Milorganite is economical, granulated for easy spreading, and comes in forty-pound bags. It lacks potash (K), so you could mix in some dehydrated manure and have a nice balanced fertilizer. If your nursery has granite dust (5 percent potash), that would mix in nicely too. My own fireplace ashes are about 7 percent potash, and they're free. If your soil test shows a severe lack of nitrogen, mix in some dried blood, which releases quickly for fast results. Or give the lawn a shot of deodorized fish fertilizer through a hose-end sprayer. If your garden center doesn't have at least these products, I'd ask the owner to order some for me. If I didn't get a response, I would go someplace else.

Milorganite, by the way, is a natural fertilizer produced specifically for lawns. It is processed sewage from the city of Milwaukee, and does have a high metal content, so make sure not to inhale it or use it near edible plants or drinking water. This product has been used for years as a slow-release, non-burning fertilizer on lawns, golf courses, and parks all across the United States. Your nursery should be able to get it.

Many natural lawn fertilizers have become available since the first release of this book. You'll find that the N-P-K numbers on the natural lawn fertilizers tend to be much lower than those on synthetic lawn fertilizers. Usually, natural fertilizers are loaded with microbes (sometimes specifically added to the mix) that will activate the soil life and make nutrients more available, with almost no waste. Additionally, many of these microbes will fight disease organisms and digest thatch (see the next chapter for more about thatch). One product, a 2-1-2 fertilizer, is advertised to accomplish the same amount of fertilizing as a 12-12-12 quick-release chemical fertilizer over the course of a growing season. This goes along with everything I've been saying about the value of natural fertilizers to soil life.

In the next chart you will see some of the materials that might be found in a natural fertilizer blend and their primary nutrient values. Some of these contain vital trace elements, too. Various methods of processing, growing, composting, and combining make each natural fertilizer unique.

If natural lawn fertilizers haven't reached the shelves of your local garden center, write to some of the sources I've listed in the Appendix. The people who run these outfits are very helpful, not just because they want to make a sale, but because they understand that part of their job is to educate others so that people will discover a better way to take care of their lawns.

There might be some unique fertilizers available in your area, due to geographical location or local industry. If these materials can be spread on a lawn, by all means use them. If not, you could try composting them or putting them in the garden. Avoid applying raw materials such as sawdust or fresh manures. Compost them or let them age first, because initially they'll take nitrogen out of the soil while they start to decompose, and later that nitrogen (plus more) will be quickly returned. The following chart will give you an idea of what your particular fertilizer contains.

HOW TO APPLY FERTILIZER

There are four common ways to spread fertilizers. I'll go over them quickly so you can see their good and bad points.

By hand. If you have a small area and an accurate toss, you can get along by doing it this way. It's very difficult, however, to spread

PERCENTAGE COMPOSITION OF COMMON ORGANIC MATERIALS

	Nitrogen	Phosphorus	Potash
Activated sludge	5.00	3.00	
Alfalfa hay	2.45	.50	2.10
Animal tankage	8.00	20.00	
Apple leaves	1.00	.15	.35
Basic slag	.80		
Blood meal	15.00	1.30	.70
Bone meal	4.00	21.00	.20
Brewer's grains (wet)	.90	.50	.05
Castor pomace	5.50	1.50	1.25
Cattle manure (fresh)	.29	.17	.35
Cocoa shell dust	1.04	1.49	2.71
Coffee grounds (dried)	1.99	.36	.67
Colloidal phosphate		18-24	
Cornstalks	.75	.40	.90
Cottonseed	3.15	1.25	1.15
Cottonseed hull ash		8.70	24.00
Cottonseed meal	7.00	2.50	1.50
Dried blood	12-15	3.00	
Feather meal	12.00		
Fish scrap (red snapper)	7.76	13.00	3.80

fertilizer evenly unless the particles you're throwing are quite large and visible on the lawn after they're thrown. I wouldn't recommend this method except for the smallest areas.

By sprayer. Homeowners normally use either a **hose-end** or a **tank sprayer**. Hose-end sprayers have a container attached to them to hold a liquid concentrate of your fertilizer, usually mixed with water according to package directions. As you spray, some of this concentrate is drawn up into the hose water through suction. The better quality hose-end sprayers work well if they're kept good and clean, but even these occasionally clog, or the suction tube takes in air near the end of the job and sprays only water. For that reason I rarely use them when a proper mixture is critical, or when spraying just

PERCENTAGE COMPOSITION OF COMMON ORGANIC MATERIALS *(continued)*

	Nitrogen	Phosphorus	Potash
Granite dust			5.00
Greensand		1.50	5.00
Guano	12.00	8.00	3.00
Hoof meal and horn dust	12.50	1.75	
Horse manure (fresh)	.44	.17	.35
Incinerator ash	.24	5.15	2.33
Leather dust	5.5-12		
Oak leaves	.80	.35	.15
Peach leaves	.90	.15	.60
Phosphate rock		30-32	
Poultry manure (fresh)	2.00	1.88	1.85
Rabbit manure (fresh)	2.40	.62	.05
Red clover	.55	.13	.50
Seaweed	1.68	.75	5.00
Sheep manure (fresh)	.55	.31	.15
Swine manure (fresh)	.60	.41	.13
Tankage	6.00	8.00	
Tobacco stems	2.00		7.00
Wood ashes		1.50	7.00

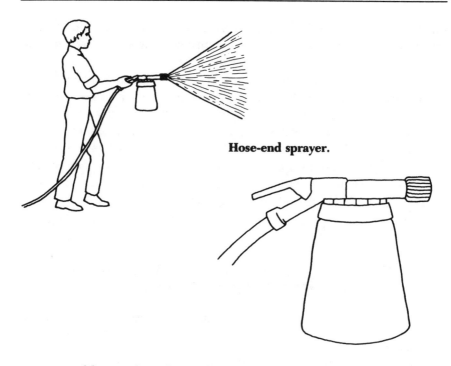

Hose-end sprayer.

water would ruin the job. For example, if I were applying a solution that was meant to stick to the grass blades, and pure water came out of the sprayer, even just for a few seconds, it would wash the solution off the blades and into the soil. For most liquid fertilizing endeavors, however, the hose-end sprayer works fine.

A **tank sprayer** distributes a solution much more accurately onto your lawn. You mix up your fertilizer with the total amount of water you plan to use (according to package directions), and then go ahead and spray. If the solution comes out at all, it will be in the right proportions. Tank sprayers are limited in the amount they can hold—rarely more than two gallons—whereas hose-end sprayers, since they hold a concentrate, are usually capable of holding the equivalent of about fifteen gallons. For most of the products the average home-owner should be using, a good hose-end sprayer will suffice. Tank sprayers are most often used for weed killer and pesticide applications, which I'm hoping you soon won't be needing.

Most liquid fertilizers are cheap, quick-release chemicals, the kind the spraying companies often use. Restrain yourself from buying them. Instead, try deodorized fish emulsion, Maxicrop (a seaweed

Tank sprayer.

fertilizer), or any similar sea product. They contain large amounts of trace elements, as well as fertilizer, growth hormones, and great amounts of helpful microorganisms. Research has shown increased disease and insect resistance on lawns treated with these sea products. Today you can find deodorized liquid cow manure and products similar to Knox Gelatin (which I use on my houseplants) in sprayable forms. An occasional application of any of these natural products can provide your soil with many benefits, including thatch decomposition.

A **drop spreader** is probably the most common and accurate tool that homeowners use for dry fertilizing. Almost every fertilizer bag has drop spreader settings listed on the back. Small adjustable holes at the bottom of the spreader allow granulated pieces to drop in about a two-foot swath.

The way you handle a lawn with one of these is first to go around the outside borders of the lawn. Then walk back and forth in straight lines, shutting the opening of the spreader as you reach the border section that was already done. When you open the spreader back up, just as you're moving off the border section, try to keep the spreader moving so that the fertilizer doesn't accumulate in one spot. Because drop spreaders are so accurate, you have to make sure that you overlap your wheels slightly with each return path you make. If you miss a spot, not even a tiny bit of the fertilizer will fall there. Drop spreaders need particles of fairly uniform size, or the small ones will drop out first.

The **broadcast spreader,** sometimes called a **rotary spreader,** has a bucket-like container on top and a whirling wheel underneath which throws the fertilizer out. The faster you walk, the farther it throws the fertilizer. This is excellent on a large lawn because you can fertilize a six-foot swath in one pass, and fairly evenly at that. It's also good because it has just one adjustable opening, meaning that you can mix large- and small-particle fertilizers, pour them in the hopper, and they'll come out mixed. With a broadcast spreader you have to fertilize on a windless day, overlapping slightly, of course, or the application will be totally inaccurate. On a very small area broadcasters can be clumsy to use. Smaller, hand-held broadcast spreaders that turn by hand crank are handy for smaller areas, or for areas where the use of wheels would make things difficult.

The problem with drop and broadcast spreaders is that everybody walks or cranks at different speeds, and your speed will determine, in part, how much fertilizer drops out of the spreader over a given area. To be safe, there are two precautions you should take. First, figure out how much fertilizer your lawn needs. Then calculate the square footage of your yard. Use a tape or pace it out, but try to be fairly accurate. Let's say you come up with 2500 square feet, and your fertilizer bag says something like, "This bag covers 5000 square feet." You obviously should use half the bag when you fertilize your lawn. The second thing you should do is set the spreader at a slightly lower rate than the bag calls for until you've tested it out on your lawn and can be sure of how true the settings are. This way you'll avoid the possibility of over-fertilizing or running out of fertilizer before you're finished.

Most lawns can be maintained beautifully with 2–4 pounds of (natural) nitrogen per 1000 square feet each year, if the soil is well structured and alive. A soil that isn't healthy has a harder time making nutrients available, and might demand slightly more fertilizer to compensate.

Always wash out a spreader after using it. Unless it's all space-age plastic, it will quickly corrode.

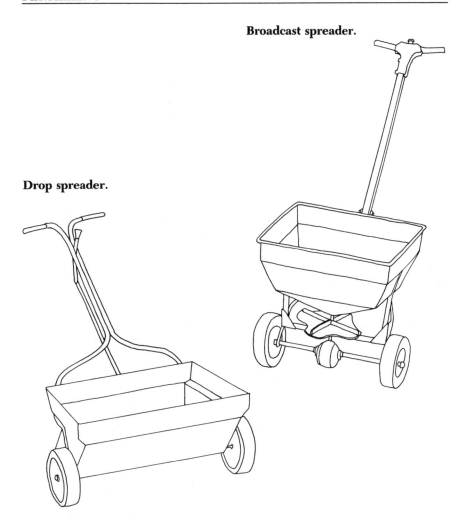

Broadcast spreader.

Drop spreader.

Important Note: Before buying a bagged lawn fertilizer, check the back of the bag to see what type of spreader is recommended. Not all natural fertilizers are granulated like their chemical counterparts, and a specific type of spreader may be required. Be sure to get this information first if purchasing by mail.

HOW MUCH FERTILIZER?

The answer to this question depends, as usual, on a number of factors. Fertilizing with the intention of building soil health is quite different from the standard chemical approach. Under ideal conditions on a well-structured, rich, living soil supporting a lawn that is mowed correctly with the clippings left on, you will need very little fertilizer. I would probably fertilize once a year with a quality blend at the recommended rate.

But you may not have ideal conditions, and bringing your soil into an ideal condition quickly might take some work. What you should concentrate on is building the soil while supplying nutrients to the grass plant. This way you will be making gradual yet long-lasting changes that will lessen your fertilizer needs in the future.

Because lawns respond best to a 4-1-2 ratio of N, P, and K, try to get close to that ratio when you fertilize. The amount of nitrogen per year that most lawns need is 2–4 pounds for every 1000 square feet (the fancy, short-cropped varieties usually need more). So if your fertilizer bag doesn't tell you how much to put on, go with the 2–4 pounds. If your lawn and soil are in bad shape, 4–6 pounds of nitrogen per 1000 square feet the first year would help. If you plan to aerate your soil, use that as a golden opportunity to get fertilizer right down into the root zone. Fertilize immediately after aerating so that some of the fertilizer will fall into the holes. Water it in right away.

Though the experts say not to use more than 1 pound of nitrogen per 1000 square feet at one application, you could put on 1½–2 pounds or more of *natural* fertilizer, especially after aerating, or when the soil and lawn are in rough shape. As an example, a bag of Milorganite 6-3-0 weighs about 40 pounds; it contains roughly 2½ pounds of nitrogen. The package says it will cover 2500 square feet on a good lawn (1 pound per 1000 square feet). However, it also says to use a double rate on a poor lawn, which means 2 pounds per 1000 square feet.

If you have a complete soil test done, you'll get a good idea of what your soil needs. Take the recommendations you receive and convert them into recommendations for natural fertilizers. Try to find a balanced natural fertilizer, or use the chart of organic materials composition (page 68) as well as any catalogs you might have to help you find a natural solution.

The importance of soil structure and soil life is now recognized in the turf industry. Products that make beneficial changes in the soil are gaining popularity. Look into the use of soil activators, conditioners, enzymes, biostimulants, and the like. Read the literature. Their use can really speed things up when you first start out.

WHEN TO FERTILIZE COOL-SEASON GRASSES

If you understand the grass plant's growth cycle, you'll know when the best fertilizing times are. In the spring, the lawn uses stored winter food to get the blades and roots started. The fast-growing foliage then produces enough food on its own to provide energy that will deepen roots and let the grass spread and thicken somewhat. When the heat comes on in late spring/early summer, the true health of the lawn becomes apparent. At this time, the lawn needs more food than it can make on its own. **It relies upon food stored away the previous fall to help it survive.** If that food isn't there, you will see weakening and damage both above and below ground. Now is when weeds, insects, disease, and draught stress can do the most damage.

When the weather gets very hot, a healthy lawn goes dormant and survives on remaining stored food. If you try to force the lawn to keep growing at this time, reserves are quickly depleted and the lawn weakens. As autumn approaches and late summer rains come, the lawn goes out of dormancy and rebuilds itself. As the weather cools down, blade growth slows down too. The grass, however, continues to produce food—more than it needs for autumn growth. So at this time, as long as the leaves are green, the grass is building up reserves—the reserves that will help it through next year's times of stress. The health of the lawn next season is, to a large degree, determined by what happens this fall.

Knowing this, you want to make sure the grass has plenty of nutrients available for early fall/late summer growth, as well as for late fall food storage. You could accomplish this with one heavy fertilizing around mid-September, but it would be better to do it in two stages. *Fertilize early in the fall, when the grass comes out of dormancy.* This will help it rebuild quickly. *Fertilize again around mid-fall, when grass growth slows up and food storage begins.* Make sure your second fertilizing is put on before temperatures are consistently low.

If the soil is too cold, soil microbes will not be as active and nutrients from the fertilizer won't be released. At this time, synthetic slow-release fertilizers, which don't depend on microbial activity, could still be used if desired.

The later fall fertilizing produces other benefits too. In the spring, the lawn will green up much earlier. But it will not force excessive growth, just normal growth. When lawns are fertilized early in the spring, they'll green up fast, but they will also grow like crazy. **Early spring fertilizing should only be done on a weak, stunted lawn that doesn't take off on its own or on a lawn that you already know is going to have problems.**

Aside from fall fertilizings, the only other time you might fertilize is middle to late spring, before it gets too hot. This will help keep good color and thicken the lawn, but it won't build up the reserves that best help grass survive the heat. DO NOT fertilize over the summer when the lawn is barely growing or is dormant. Only the weeds will benefit from summer fertilizing.

WHEN TO FERTILIZE WARM-SEASON GRASSES

Lawns in the South should be fertilized differently than northern lawns. They do not go dormant in the summertime, but actually grow more aggressively. Cool spring and fall weather slows their growth, and the winter is their dormant time (though winter is an active time for weeds in the South).

The Cooperative Extension Service advises against late fall fertilizing on warm-season grasses, especially in the cooler, transitional areas of the country. It makes warm-season grasses more prone to winterkill. Additionally, this late fall fertilizing will sprout and encourage weed growth while the grass is dormant.

Fertilize heavily in mid-spring as your main application. You could break fertilizing up into early and late spring applications. Fertilize lightly again in midsummer, because the grass will be using up many nutrients during its active summer growth. A schedule of April-June-August (with natural fertilizers) is safe for most warm-season grasses.

7 ◆ THATCH

People have the erroneous idea that if they leave their clippings on the lawn, these clippings will turn into thatch. That is not usually the case. In fact, clippings are only a small part of the picture. Thatch is actually an interwoven mass of stolons, stems, rhizomes, roots, leaf blades, and sheaths all sitting on top of the soil surface. Thatch has become a major lawn problem in modern-day lawns. It is often a result of poor lawn care practices by both the homeowner and the lawn pro.

If you poke your finger down through your grass, it should go into the soil quite easily. If you find a barrier about ½–¾ inches or more of matted grass parts, you have thatch. You'll be able to feel it. A thin layer of grass clippings is nothing to worry about. It is the thicker part of the plant that weaves the thatch layer.

WHAT'S WRONG WITH THATCH?

Everything! It absorbs water and fertilizers before they reach the soil; it prevents air from reaching the soil; it becomes a breeding ground for insects and disease; it can suffocate the grass and squeeze it out. But most importantly, it becomes the medium of growth for more stolons and rhizomes, and eventually roots. In other words, the roots grow into the thatch (where the water and perhaps the fertilizer is) instead of the soil. You end up with a lawn growing on top of the soil instead of into the soil. This makes the grass highly susceptible to dehydration, frost, and traffic and insect damage.

And here's more: thatch is soft and spongy, which makes mowing difficult when the wheels sink in. It scalps easily and can repel water when it dries out.

You can expect the stoloniferous grasses such as bentgrass, Bermuda, St. Augustine, and zoysia to form thatch easily because they send shoots out above ground. If these shoots start weaving around each other, and they keep the grass clippings from the soil, they will soon create thatch. Lawn grasses that spread only by rhizomes should not have the same problem.

HOW TO CREATE THATCH ON ANY LAWN

First, give the lawn quick-release nitrogen so there is excessive topgrowth that can't decompose quickly enough. The fast-release fertilizer will also kill off some valuable soil life that would help decompose thatch material.

Next, keep your lawn cut short so that its roots stay near the top of the soil. A hard-compacted soil will keep roots short, too.

Water lightly, but often. Keep only the top of the soil moist, so the roots will reach upward for water.

Treat the lawn with pesticides and fungicides to chase away worms and other soil life.

As the soil life is leaving, clippings and stems will decompose even more slowly. Fertilizer will sit on top of the developing thatch layer. The roots and rhizomes (and stolons, if your grass type has them) will work their way up and make more thatch. Within a season or two, you can develop a nice layer of thatch.

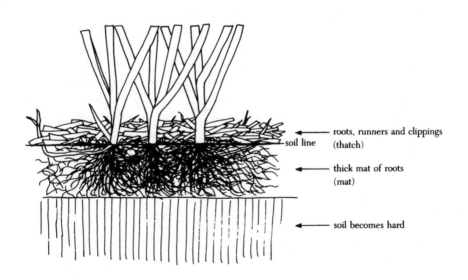

soil line — roots, runners and clippings (thatch)

— thick mat of roots (mat)

— soil becomes hard

HANDLING A THATCH PROBLEM

A serious case of thatch can take years to form. Its complete removal can take years, too, but there are ways to speed the process. Whatever else you do, have the long-range intention of creating a rich, living, and porous soil in which decomposition occurs rapidly and roots penetrate deeply. Take these steps immediately:

- While handling a thatch problem, catch the grass clippings so they don't add to it.
- Apply a natural soil conditioner.
- Change your watering practices: water deeply and let the thatch area get *slightly* dry. Encourage the roots to go down. If water won't penetrate the thatch or a compacted, hard-to-wet soil, do a soap treatment before or with each watering.
- Core-Aerate the lawn. I'd do this at least twice a year, in spring and early fall. The core aerator pokes 2–3 inches or deeper (the deeper the better) holes into the soil and throws out the cores as it moves along. The cores eventually break down into the lawn. Without damaging a lawn, an aerator provides instant holes for air, water, fertilizer, and roots.

  Go over the lawn twice, making holes 4–6 inches apart. Be sure to water the soil the night before so the aerator can penetrate as deeply as possible. Rent a machine with a neighbor or two and it will be cheap.

  Aerating goes very fast, and it is probably one of the best things you can do for any lawn. My favorite trick is to aerate each September and follow immediately with a heavy fertilizing. I water afterward to get some of the fertilizer down into the soil, where the roots are supposed to be. This leads us to our next step.
- Get some *life* into the thatch layer and the soil. You are not too interested in anything that will produce a lot of new growth. You want bacteria to decompose aboveground dead or decaying matter. Any of the high quality organic fertilizer blends will work well. Try sea products, liquid manure (deodorized), or even a quart of beer through your hose-end sprayer. These will also help to restore life to the soil, open it up for drainage and root growth, and bring back earthworms.

  Good soil conditioners, such as Vita-Flow (Green Pro Services) or

Aerating machine.

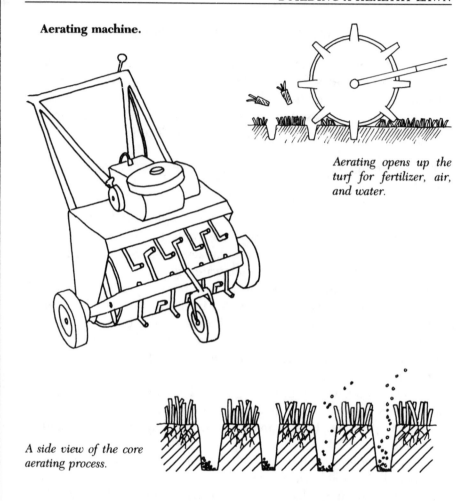

Aerating opens up the turf for fertilizer, air, and water.

A side view of the core aerating process.

Nitron A-35 (Nitron Industries Inc.) are much more effective than just soap and water. Not only do they allow water to pass through the thatch and penetrate deeply, but they add the enzymes and bacteria that help decompose aboveground decaying plant matter. They bring about more life within the soil as well. Use a conditioner three times over the course of the season for fastest results.

It is entirely possible to rid your lawn of thatch within a two-to-three-year period without mechanical removal, if you use proper natural lawn care techniques, soil conditioners, and fertilizers that contain proper microlife. You won't need to aerate, either. A lawn growing in a healthy living soil with proper structure aerates itself.

There are a couple of other machines besides an aerator that can assist you:

The **power rake** is useful on light cases of thatch, or when clippings are building up. The steel tines are strong, but they can't break up a thick thatch layer.

The **vertical mower** uses metal blades that slice through the thatch and thin it out, bringing it to the surface. The blades should be set deep enough to get just under the thatch layer. The amount of thatch that gets pulled out can be amazing. If you find that the machine is ripping the lawn right off the soil, stop the machine—your thatch has caused such shallow rooting that the grass can't take vertical mowing. You could try setting the blades higher so they just break the thatch up a bit. Frequent aerating should be done (as well as all the other steps) before you attempt vertical mowing again.

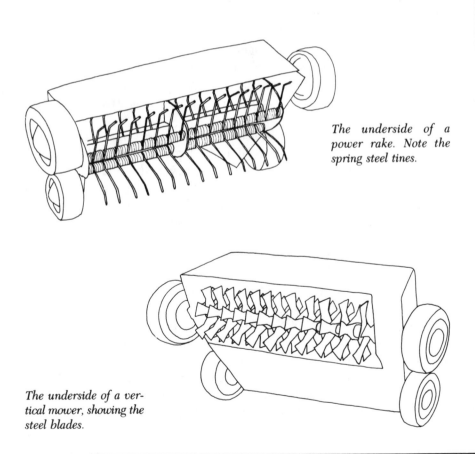

The underside of a power rake. Note the spring steel tines.

The underside of a vertical mower, showing the steel blades.

8♦TYPES OF GRASSES

Each region of the country supports certain grasses that grow best there. Knowing the specific type or types of grass in your lawn will help you determine how to care for it. If you are planning a new lawn, you should learn about the particular qualities and demands of any grass before you plant it.

You can classify a lawn grass as either a **cool-season** or **warm-season** grass. Cool-season grasses grow best in the northern climates, and thrive at temperatures averaging 60–80 degrees F. They survive freezing winter temperatures, but can't take truly hot weather for long without going dormant. Often, two or more different types of cool-season grasses will grow well together.

Cool-season grasses can be planted over a warm-season lawn in the South as **wintergrass** to keep the lawn green during colder weather. As soon as the weather warms up, the warm-season grasses take over again.

Provided there is enough moisture, cool-season grasses will grow in most of the northern states as well as the higher elevations and coastal areas where temperatures are cooler. However, there are some areas of the northern states, Canada, the plains, and the mountains that are too tough or dry for a nice cool-season lawn. The grasses that will grow in these places are what you might call **native grasses.** These are the same grasses found growing wild on the range and the prairie.

Warm-season grasses thrive in areas with hot summers and mild winters. They go dormant and usually turn brown from late fall to early spring, hence the use of wintergrass by those who want green the year round. Warm-season grasses are aggressive and don't mix well together, as many of the cool-season grasses do. One grass type will quickly take over. Most warm-season grasses don't survive extremely cold temperatures, so you will rarely find them in the north.

The next thing to know is that grasses can be **fine-bladed** (thin and fairly soft-to-the-touch), or **coarse** (wider and rough-to-the-touch). Most long-standing home lawns were originally intended to be fine-

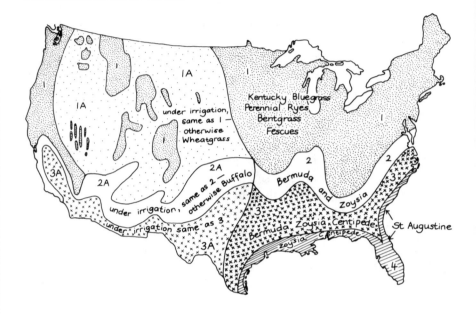

bladed, though the coarse types have often snuck in and taken over. You'll notice patches of coarse grass sticking up in clumps, especially in midsummer when the other grasses might be dormant or growing very slowly.

The third fact you need to know has to do with the way the grass grows and spreads. This was touched upon earlier in chapter 2. Grasses spread in four ways.

1. Tillers—new shoots to the original plant added at the base. Grasses that spread this way are sometimes called **clump grasses,** but this is often a derogatory term saved for thick-bladed, large clumping types.

2. Rhizomes—underground stems that form new plants within a few inches of the mother plant. Grasses that spread primarily by rhizomes are usually very upright and easy to care for.

3. Stolons—aboveground stems that root and then send up new shoots along their length. Most of the warm-season grasses spread this way, as well as the bentgrasses in the North. They are very aggressive grasses that can easily choke out other types. Their aboveground spreading habit gives them a strong tendency to knit together and cause thatch.

4. Seeds—most grasses will go to seed if they're not cut short, but some won't. This becomes an important factor when you are concerned with putting in a new lawn or filling in bare spots.

Finally, you should understand that some grasses are **annuals,** growing for one season before they die, and that other grasses are **perennials,** which theoretically go on forever. The annual grasses usually sprout fast, and are often included in seed mixtures to start something growing quickly that will provide shade and protection for the slow-sprouting permanent seeds. When used in mixtures for this purpose they are called **nurse grasses** or **companion grasses.**

What you probably would like on your lawn is a fine-bladed, perennial grass lawn. Maybe that's exactly what you have already. An experienced landscaper or nursery person could tell you at a glance what is growing in your lawn, but to help you identify your grass type yourself and understand some of the special qualities different varieties have, I am going to give a summary of some of the popular grasses. Once you're familiar with these, you might be able to see what is best suited to your yard's particular growing conditions. The Lawn Institute, P.O. Box 108, Pleasant Hill, Tennessee 38578 can help you select the grass type and variety best suited to your area. Explain your situation and send a legal size self-addressed, stamped envelope requesting the special topic sheet on the current "Grass Seed Recognition List."

THE COOL-SEASON GRASSES

Annual ryegrass. Here is one you have to be very careful about purchasing. A package of grass seed that says "Quick Grow" or "Super Fast" probably contains all or part annual ryegrass. Realize that though this lawn will germinate in only a few days, it will die over the winter in colder climates and leave bare or thin spots. Annual rye has a medium-to-coarse leaf blade, adds tillers, and gets clumpy over its one season of growth. It is the primary grass type planted in the fall in warm-season lawns, where it grows as a wintergrass. Its deep-rooting quality helps loosen up heavier soils.

In the cool-season grass areas annual ryegrass is sometimes used as a companion, or nurse grass, in a seed mixture to help the perennial grass establish itself. For example, bluegrass might take three weeks to germinate. If you mix some annual rye seed with the bluegrass seed, the quick-sprouting annual rye will shade the bluegrass seed, keep the soil from caking up, and allow you to do less babysitting of your newly seeded lawn.

You can expect to find less annual rye in the perennial rye seed mixtures of the future. Improved perennial ryes will sprout quickly enough to establish their place in, and remain part of, a lawn.

Bentgrass. Cut a quarter-inch high, bentgrass is used on putting greens. When it's allowed to grow higher than about one inch, trouble can be expected. It gets high when it's seeded thickly or when it's in competition with upright grasses, and tends to mat up in a sideways growth pattern of stolons and blades, discolored except at the very top. It is shallow-rooted and forms thatch easily.

Bentgrass in an upright lawn is likely to choke out the other grasses eventually. Many people consider it a weed and try to eliminate it before it eliminates the rest of their lawn.

Bentgrass does best in full sun. Because it is shallow-rooted it needs extra fertilizing, and the very top of the soil must stay moist. These conditions can create the disease problems with which bentgrass has become associated. If you rake your lawn and find some sideways stems lifting up six or eight inches, that's bentgrass. Keep it lifted straight and it won't look too bad.

Chewing fescue is very similar to creeping fescue, except that it can be cut lower and might form clumps. It can be mixed with shorter growing improved bluegrass. Both chewing and red fescue have minimal fertilizer needs.

Colonial bentgrass. This type probably looks best when cut ¾–1 inch high. It creates an attractive lawn but requires extra mowing, fertilizing, and general maintenance to make up for its short height and shallow roots. It spreads by aboveground stolons, and you can expect some thatch accumulation. It can be mixed with fine fescues, but not with any other grasses. In cool and misty coastal climates with acid soils, it will make a picture-perfect lawn.

Creeping fescue, or **red fescue**, isn't red, nor does it really creep—it spreads by rhizomes. It is fine-bladed and thin with rather rounded blades, grows well in medium shade and dry soils, and looks very nice when cut high. It is deep green and mixes well in sunny areas with common bluegrass. If you plant creeping fescue alone, in a shady area for instance, be sure not to trample it much. It is not as durable as most other grass types.

Kentucky bluegrass. This is the most common fine-bladed lawn grass, the standard other grasses are measured by. Although there are dozens of bluegrass varieties, you can simplify the subject by dividing them into common Kentucky bluegrass and improved Kentucky bluegrass. The improved, hybrid varieties (Merion, Nugget, Windsor, Adelphi, Fylking, to name a few) are a little more disease-resistant than common. Some can be mowed shorter than other bluegrasses. Some are a darker green than usual. Some, especially Merion (which is susceptible to rust disease), need more fertilizer and more babying than common bluegrass. Sod lawns are often blends of a few improved varieties. Common bluegrass can take more neglect than the improved varieties, and still look good.

Bluegrass, as a rule, does not do well in the shade or in dry conditions. It spreads by underground stems (rhizomes) to form new plants close to the mother plant. It should be cut high (at least three inches), especially during the summer. More than once I've seen a beautiful bluegrass sod lawn ruined in a single season by continual low cutting.

Bluegrass lawns require 2–4 pounds of nitrogen per 1000 square feet each season, about average for most lawn types. This doesn't all have to come from fertilizers. Clippings, soil life, and all the natural fertilizing processes count, too.

Perennial ryegrass (turf-type). This seems to be getting more popular, and new varieties are constantly being developed. Their colors are deeper green and have better resistance to insects and disease than many other popular grasses.

Ryegrasses germinate (sprout) very quickly, and wear well. The more popular varieties, such as Pennfine and Manhattan, blend in well with bluegrass, and give a nice cut. Their fertilizer needs are average. They do not send out rhizomes or stolons, so bare and thin spots have to be reseeded.

Tall fescue (Kentucky 31, Fawn, Alta) is a wide, rough-bladed grass. It grows in clumps that get larger and larger and that will take over a fine-bladed lawn. You can cut your finger on it if you rub it just right. This is often advertised as playground grass because it is very tough, and it is often planted along roadsides. Because it takes hot weather, it is used in transition areas, where the weather is not quite right for either cool-season or warm-season grasses.

Clumps of this type of grass in a fine-bladed lawn can slow up the lawn mower. It should be cut high, 3–4 inches minimum, and has average fertilizer needs. Tall fescue is mistakenly called crabgrass by many homeowners who don't want it in their lawn. If you don't need a tough grass like tall fescue, you probably don't want it.

Turf-type tall fescue is a fairly recent addition to the grass seed market. The Lawn Institute Special Topic Sheet describes it as having finer leaf blades and more resistance to insects and disease than older types. It grows better in shade and acid conditions than most grasses, and makes better use of soil moisture and nutrients than any other lawn grass. These are strong recommendations for a durable grass that might grow where others won't. The Lawn Institute singles out these turf-type tall fescues as the best for 1986: Clemfine and Rebel (Loft's Inc.), Falcon (E. F. Burlingham & Sons), Galway (Northrup King), Houndog (International Seeds Inc.), and Mustang (Pickseed West). Write to the Lawn Institute for the most updated listings.

The Native Grasses. As mentioned earlier, these are not used for lush green home lawns. They grow out on the range and the prairies and near the mountains, where they prevent erosion and keep the ground covered with some greenery where conditions are too tough for a typical lawn.

The two most popular native grasses are **Fairway Wheatgrass (Agropyron)** and **Buffalograss**. Wheatgrass is a cool-season type, while buffalograss behaves more like a warm-season type. Wheatgrass grows in western Canada and in the plains and mountain areas of the U.S. It will withstand extremes of temperatures, though it prefers colder, drier weather and alkaline soils. Buffalograss grows best just south of where wheatgrass grows. It grows during the hot summer with little need for water, and goes dormant as soon as the weather turns cold. It is a finer bladed grass than wheatgrass, and can make a dense, grey-green lawn, able to be maintained at shorter heights. You'll see buffalograss left uncut on roadsides and low-maintenance areas.

Though not the most attractive lawn types, the native grasses will produce a thick covering. They require mowing only about once a month. Other cool-season grasses will grow in the native grass regions if you provide an extra 4–5 inches of water per month.

THE WARM-SEASON GRASSES

Bahiagrass, another coarse-bladed variety, is also adaptable to coastal areas where finer grasses won't take. In some lawns it would be considered a weed, but its thick root network makes it a strong lawn where erosion is a problem. It spreads aboveground by stolons, and forms a loose-looking turf. It handles shade quite well. Cut high, with average fertilizer and water applications, Bahiagrass will create an economical lawn where fine grass isn't needed.

Bermudagrass is to southern lawns what bluegrass is to northern lawns—it is the main grass type. When given care it grows vigorously, crowding out other grasses and weeds, and filling in bare spots. Common Bermuda can be planted from seed, but the improved varieties are planted as **sprigs**. Sprigs are individual stems, rhizomes, or stolons which are planted at intervals and eventually fill in to form a lawn.

Bermudagrass can be cut low if given extra care, but at greater cutting heights it is easy to maintain. It doesn't have high water requirements, but should not be allowed to dry out completely in the midsummer heat. It doesn't do well in shade. You must fertilize Bermudagrass more than most grasses, and keep an eye out for thatch formation, which is common in the varieties that spread by stolons. Some varieties spread by rhizomes, too.

Centipedegrass requires little maintenance, but is not the most beautiful of grasses. It adapts to many soil conditions, resists chinch bugs and many diseases, grows aggressively enough to crowd out

Left page: *Two views of how common weeds can enhance a lawn at certain times of the year.* **Top:** *Dandelions. Photo by Alan H. Graham, f/STOP Pictures.* **Bottom:** *Creeping speedwell. Photo by Ann Reilly.*

Right page: *Less attractive weeks as they look in the lawn.* **Top:** *White clover:* **Right:** *Ground ivy.* **Bottom:** *Crabgrass seedlings. Photos courtesy of the New York State Turfgrass Association.*

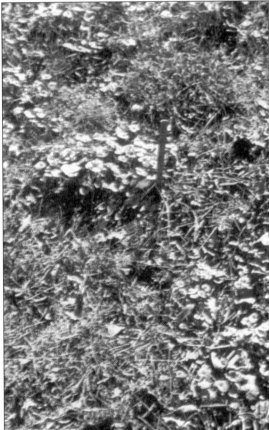

Left page. Top left: *Severe grub damage.* Top right: *Grubs under the sod.* Bottom: *Skunks have dug up this lawn in pursuit of grubs. Photos courtesy of the New York State Turfgrass Association.*

Right page. Top: *Chinch bug damage. Photo Courtesy of the New York State Turfgrass Association.* Bottom: *Fusarium disease. Photo courtesy of Ringer Corporation.*

Left page: *The effects of improper mowing.* **Top:** *Scalping.* **Bottom:** *One side of this lawn was mown with a dull blade, the other side with a sharp blade. Photos by Stuart Franklin*

Right page: Right: *Raking, particularly in spring and fall, is not just for aesthetics; it is an important preventive medicine for lawns. Photo by Jerry Howard, Positive Images.* **Bottom:** *Thatch layer (left) on lawn compared with a thatch-free layer. Photo courtesy of Ringer Corporation.* **Middle:** *Most grasses won't survive directly under a tree, where they have to compete with the tree's above-ground roots for survival. Pachysandra and other ground covers are good solutions. Photo by Jerry Howard, Positive Images.*

A healthy lawn is a happy place for plants, animals, and people. Photo by Jerry Howard, Positive Images.

weeds, needs less mowing and fertilizing than fancier lawns, and will tolerate some shade. However, the blades are not a deep green and are on the coarse side. It has short roots, and so needs more water than most grasses. Centipedegrass grows best in the southern half of the warm-season grass regions.

St. Augustinegrass is a thick-bladed variety that is the best choice for shaded areas. It forms a dense but rather spongy turf which, though not durable enough for a play or sports surface, makes an attractive lawn where finer types can't be grown. St. Augustine is sold inexpensively as sod in southern coastal areas, and shows a high tolerance to salt. It spreads by thick aboveground stolons and should be kept three inches high (except for dwarf varieties). Thatch is not a major problem if the lawn is given an occasional raking to remove any build-up. Chinch bugs are a problem on St. Augustine, however. (See how to handle in *Insects* section.) Seed is not available for St. Augustine, so lawns are installed or repaired by using sod, plugs, or sprigs.

Zoysiagrass is advertised as the "miracle grass" you plug into your lawn. The **plugs** are simply small sections of zoysia sod that root slowly and then spread over your lawn in three to four years. Its dense growth—spreading by both stolons and rhizomes—crowds out most other grasses, as well as most weeds. It takes the sun, but doesn't do well at all in the shade. You don't have to mow this slow-growing grass often, and it is quite resistant to insects and diseases.

Zoysiagrass can be used in many of the northern states, though in colder areas it doesn't have a long growing season. In western New York zoysiagrass doesn't green up until mid-spring, and goes dormant again in October. The frustrating part about its dormancy is that it turns straw colored, standing out in any neighborhood where cool-season lawns stay fairly green throughout their winter dormancy.

If you live in the Northern states or Canada and don't mind zoysiagrass's short season and straw color when dormant, it will make you an easy-to-care-for lawn. Zoysia, despite its ability to survive colder temperatures, is more of a warm-season grass, and is used extensively in the southern states. Once established, it needs little water, and its fertilizer requirements are on the low side. It develops into a very thick, wear-resistant lawn that also can be cut short (down to three-fourths of an inch) or left at two inches. Thatch is almost unavoidable on zoysiagrass lawns, but it doesn't seem to cause as many problems on zoysia as it might on other lawns.

LAWNS OF THE FUTURE

Today's lawn grasses have been genetically engineered for such qualities as insect and disease resistance, root strength, pleasing color, drought tolerance, and many more desirable attributes. One of the most interesting areas of lawn grass research is the isolation of chemicals that are emitted by certain grasses which can repel or kill weeds, insects, and disease. Not only will better grasses emerge from this research, but possibly new natural lawn-care products will emerge as well.

Plant geneticist Jan Weijer was in the news in 1986 with developments of grasses (derived from native alpine species) that not only resist weeds and diseases, but need little sun, water, or fertilizer—and they grow only 2½–6 inches a summer. These should be available commercially very soon.

BUYING YOUR GRASS SEED

Some lawn grasses can be grown only from sprigs, plugs, or sod. But for the majority of grass types seed is still available.

If you plan to seed a lawn soon, you should understand how seed is sold and why. Typically, you will find grass seed sold as a **mixture,** a **blend,** or a **straight** type. Mixtures, two or more grass types together, commonly consist of bluegrass, fescue, and annual rye. A blend is two or more varieties, called **cultivars,** of the same type of grass. Bluegrass blends might contain these three cultivars: Nugget bluegrass, Windsor bluegrass, and Fylking bluegrasses. A straight seed is exactly one type and cultivar of grass. The warm-season grasses are almost always sold as straight seed because one of these grass types would thoroughly dominate another within a season. The cool-season grasses are usually sold as mixtures.

WHICH GRASS IS FOR YOU?

The grasses in a mixture are often fairly similar in appearance, but can adapt to a variety of conditions. The bluegrass-fescue-annual rye mix I mentioned would do well in a yard that was mostly sunny with some areas of light shade. In the shady, drier, or wetter areas the fescue would predominate. The bluegrass would respond to the full sun and better soil. Neither would totally overgrow the other unless conditions went to extremes; the lawn would adjust from season to season. If insects or disease attacked one grass, the other would probably fill in.

Blends or straights might look a little better, but they carry the potential of getting wiped out if a particular disease attacks. They are best used for specific, fairly constant conditions, or for fancy lawns one is willing to keep a close eye on.

When the time comes to choose your seed, knowledgeable nursery keepers are your best friends. They can recommend the correct prepackaged mixture, or might be able to mix a custom one for you. They'll know how to read a seed package label and will tell you exactly what it means.

If you can't get this kind of expert help, I'll give you a few guidelines. If you are buying a mixture, go with a name brand company, or an exact duplicate in type and quality. There are many ways for an unscrupulous company to throw in inferior seed. Read each package carefully. Screen out any that say tall fescue (Kentucky 31 fescue) unless you want it. Check to see if there is annual ryegrass,

GRASS SEED CHARACTERISTICS

	Seeds Per Pound	Pounds Per 1000 Square Feet	Days to Germination
Annual ryegrass	220,000	8–9	8
Bahiagrass	180,000	8	18–28
Bermudagrass (common)	180,000	2	7–28
Bentgrass (creeping)	6,000,000	1–2	12–28
Buffalograss	300,000	5	20–30
Centipedegrass	400,000	½	18
Fescue (fine)	600,000	4–5	10–21
Fescue (tall)	250,000	8	10–21
Kentucky bluegrass (common)	2,200,000	1½–2	7–28
Perennial ryegrass	230,000	8–9	7
Poa trivialis	2,200,000	1–2	10–28

and if so, how much. The percentages of seed blends and mixtures go by weight, not by number of seeds. Four pounds of a 50 percent bluegrass-50 percent ryegrass mix means 4,400,000 bluegrass seeds and only 460,000 ryegrass seeds. Interesting, isn't it? Look to see if there is a recommended spreader setting for seeding. Figuring this out yourself by experimentation could cost you half your seeds.

Don't get stuck planting the wrong type of grass! Once it's growing, grass can't easily be removed. Don't buy seed that is old, or doesn't have a label available. Even the loose, bulk seed in hardware store bins comes in labeled sacks, so ask to see a label before buying. A store's "problem lawn" mixture might turn out to be all tall fescue and weed seed. Reputable storeowners will carry good mixes from reputable seed growers. Discount grass seed is rarely a bargain in the long run. Seed from a good nursery or garden center, even if it costs a little more, is a sound investment.

As a final word, before you decide to reseed or sod an area, try to determine why the previous lawn didn't do well. I've seen more lawns ruined by short cutting than anything else, but improper watering methods, poor soil, excessive chemicals, and inappropriate grass types should be examined as reasons for lawn failure.

9♦SEEDING A LAWN

Why do some people have so much difficulty getting their grass seed to grow into a lawn? Over the years I have become very familiar with the lament, "I can't get grass seed to grow." This is a curious problem, since the great purpose of any seed is to sprout and grow. Seeds certainly do well enough in the places where you don't want them.

SPROUTING COMES FIRST

If you can't get the grass seed to sprout, you won't have a chance for a lawn. And if you don't take care of the grass correctly after it sprouts, you'll be disappointed as you watch your new lawn disappear before it becomes established.

Because sprouting comes first, let's begin with the two factors which have to exist regardless of anything else: moisture and warmth. In nature, a seed knows innately that it's safe to open up during the moist, warm days of mid-spring and late summer–early fall. If there is a likelihood of the soil drying out or chilling, the seed stays put, which is why many seeds stay dormant during the hot and dry days of summer. Though grass seeds will sprout in hot and wet soil, these conditions are highly conducive to weeds, insects, and disease. So do yourself a favor and hold off on seeding during the summer. Wait until the weather breaks (late August to mid-September). If you need a lawn fast, put down some pre-grown grass–sod.

Some people seed in early spring or early fall, and then let nature take its course. You can help this process along by maintaining consistent soil moisture. In other words, you'll get faster germination if you water the newly seeded area as soon as you notice that the soil is drying out. Every yard has different conditions, of course, and it's up to you to decide how your yard's conditions affect the soil moisture. Factors such as shade, wind, tree root water absorption, soil type, and slope play their part in determining how moist the soil is. Mulching with straw or peat moss will hold moisture in, but will not substitute for regular watering. If you can keep the soil consistently moist without drowning the seed, germination will be quick.

SOIL AND AIR TEMPERATURE

The second determining factor for seed germination is soil and air warmth. In spring the warmth of the air and sunlight work to heat up the soil, and the cool-season grasses will slowly germinate as the soil thaws out. When the soil temperature reaches about 50 degrees (mid-spring), grass will germinate at a more normal rate. At 60 degrees soil warmth (late spring), grass seed will germinate extremely fast, often in as little as four or five days, depending on the seed type. Of course, there must be sufficient moisture as well.

TIMING YOUR SEEDING

It would seem that mid-to-late spring would be the best time to seed. But with both cool- and warm-season grasses, you can run into difficulties with mid-to-late spring seeding. First of all, a lawn seeded at that time might not establish itself soon enough to withstand the summer heat that cool-season grasses hate. And second, crabgrass and undesirable weeds begin to sprout when the soil temperature starts warming up to 60 degrees. If any of these seeds are in your soil, they'll quickly dominate the newly seeded area. By seeding in the *early* spring, you can encourage a thick and tall stand of grass before the soil warms up to 60 degrees, and you'll prevent these weedgrasses from growing.

By far the best time to seed all grass types is late August to mid-September, when the soil is nice and warm yet the air has cooled down from summer temperatures. Weeds are not as active at this time, and the soil isn't soggy, as you often find it in the spring.

Whenever you do choose to seed, remember that different seed types germinate at different times. The slower ones should be planted earlier. In general, the annual and perennial ryes are the fastest of the cool-season grasses, bluegrasses are the slowest, and the fescues and bentgrasses are somewhere in between. Although many southern lawns are planted from sod, sprigs, or plugs (see chapter 10, *Sod Lawns*), seeding is still common. Bermudagrass seeds generally sprout fastest, and zoysiagrass slowest. Warm-season grasses generally take longer to germinate.

One or more types of seed in a fall-seeded lawn might not germinate if the weather turns cold too quickly. The seed should stay dormant and sprout the following spring with perhaps a 20 percent seed loss due to age, rot, and other unavoidable factors. It would be safer to plant seed in November, and let it stay dormant all winter, than to seed in mid-October and get the grass to germinate just as winter hits. The tender new plants, especially in the North, are susceptible to damage from extreme temperature, as well as to being heaved out of the ground by the freezing and thawing action of the soil.

Remember, grass seed needs both moisture and warmth in order to sprout. Without moisture it surely won't do a thing. There is more leeway with temperature. Grass seed might germinate slowly under cooler temperatures, but quickly when it is warm. If there is evidence of a lack of moisture or warmth coming on, the seed will usually remain dormant.

Once the lawn seed has germinated it will be very sensitive until the roots dig in and the plants become established. Do not walk over the young grass. And most important, keep the soil moist until all the seeds are established—the new plants can dry out and die in a matter of hours. This is why summer seeding is so tough. And seeding a mix of different grasses can be tricky, too. For instance, the bluegrass seed in a mix might not germinate for ten days after the rest of the seeds. If you have stopped watering by then, you may never see your bluegrass. **Ordinarily, you should not keep the soil surface moist, but seeding time is the exception to this rule.**

You can usually tell moist soil by its darker color. But the sun and wind can dry out the surface, where the seeds are, very quickly. If you sow the seeds deeper than a half-inch, they might stay moist longer, but probably won't sprout because seeds also need air in order to sprout. You could sow seed right on top of the ground under the best of conditions, but most of us will need to plant the seed about a quarter-inch deep to keep it constantly moist. A light mulch of peat moss or straw (not hay, which hasn't had the seeds threshed out) will conserve moisture and prevent evaporation. It can also keep rain or sprinkler water from washing away seeds.

See the ground in front of you. Your particular soil, temperature, and moisture conditions will dictate when and how to go about seeding.

AVOID THESE MISTAKES

Even if you are blessed with the right temperature and moisture conditions, there are still ways to mess up. **The most common mistake is too little seed.** The experts say 15–20 seeds per square inch is about right. This is slightly less than three million seeds per 1000 square feet—a thick lawn even if only half the seeds sprout. Don't skimp on seed! A thin lawn will need more care, and will provide plenty of space for weeds to grow in.

Another mistake is **using old seed**. Typically, only about 80–90 percent of your seed will germinate. If the seed is from the previous year, that percentage may drop drastically. Seed that is kept refrigerated or stored in a cold, dark place will last longer. If you are using older seed, make sure you put it on more heavily—maybe 1 ½ times the normal amount. Some seeds will last for decades or longer under the right conditions, but don't expect that to hold true with your old lawn seed.

Using the wrong type of seed can cause untold difficulties. The chapter on the different types of grasses covers the subject of choosing your seed. A sun-loving grass planted in a shady area will be a great failure. Seeing your new lawn come up with rough meadow grass instead of the fine-bladed grass you imagined can be depressing, to say the least. Decide what type of grass you want and check to make sure that it fits into the conditions of your yard. Ask the staff at your local nursery to recommend a variety.

I once checked over the grass seed selection at a popular discount store, and found that out of four choices, only the fanciest seed was suitable for a normal lawn in the store's area. The other three were mostly quick-growing annual ryes, or rough-bladed tall fescues. Every year thousands of people trust the name of the seed or the picture on the package, and end up with a problem lawn.

Using bargain seed: choosing your seed by the price tag is usually a mistake. The cheapest seed will contain the largest amount of annual or rough-bladed grasses. If you want that kind of grass, you're lucky it's cheap, but the better lawn seeds are a little more expensive. By the pound, Kentucky bluegrass appears to be the most expensive of the common cool-season grasses, but because its seeds are so small, it turns out to be one of the cheapest. One pound of bluegrass seed covers as much area as four pounds of other types. And because bluegrass seed doesn't even cost twice as much as other fine-bladed seed, it works out to be an economical seed choice.

The last common seeding error I'd like to mention is **poor soil preparation.** We'll cover this in detail in the next section. For now it's sufficient to say that without a decent soil to grow in, any seed will have a rough time of it. Take care of your soil and it will support a beautiful lawn.

SEEDING METHODS

Now that you know what it takes for a seed to sprout and then to survive, we can go over the exact methods of putting seed down. Seeded correctly and at the right time, a thick lawn will practically spring from the soil. Seeded incorrectly, your lawn will be a patch of dirt, scattered weeds, and an occasional wisp of grass.

PREPARING FOR THE NEW LAWN

Putting in a new lawn usually means either working with an unlandscaped yard or replacing an existing lawn. **Careful preparation will save future work and expense.** If you are planting in the yard of a new home, make sure you get all construction debris out of the soil. Rotting wood can cause mushrooms and dips in the soil; cement and other man-made materials can create chemical reactions in the soil. If you are worried about this, mix a generous amount of gypsum into the soil to help neutralize any chemicals. Don't leave pockets of sand or gravel unless they are buried very deeply. Water will drain through these pockets too fast and you'll end up with dry areas and spots of trouble in your lawn. Clean out the yard and then determine what kind of soil you are left with.

Next, consider the **grade,** or **slope,** of the lawn. A gentle slope away from the house will keep surface water from basement walls. Your builder probably graded the land this way when he finished construction. If he didn't, and it's too late to have it graded, you had better be sure to install **drain tile** or some other water drainage system. Most new homes are waterproofed around the foundation, but without some system for draining the water away, there can still be trouble. If you suspect that your lawn area will have trouble drying out, you should consider putting drain tile right in the lawn. Seek out several professional opinions, and check with your town's water department before proceeding.

Obviously, a complete soil test is the best way to determine whether your soil needs lime or other nutrients. But you can determine a lot by simple observation. Do you have topsoil, or something more like a clay subsoil? Is there any sign of soil life? What kind of weeds are growing, and what do they tell you about the soil? (See chapter 13, *Weed Control*.) Is the soil loose? Muddy? Sandy? Check the clay/sand/silt content with the simple water-and-soil-in-a-jar test described in chapter 5.

The safest preparation of any but an ideal soil is the addition of organic matter, or some good soil, or both. Then mix in some organic fertilizer and you'll be ready for seeding. Remember, your soil structure will be maintained by the life in the soil, which feeds on decaying organic matter.

Let's assume that you have about four inches of questionable topsoil sitting on a clay subsoil. Using a rototiller, you can mix in peat moss, grass clippings, manures, leaves, sawdust, and plenty of organic fertilizer. An inch or two of organic matter, thoroughly turned into the top six inches of soil, will help develop the nutrient-rich, living soil you are working for.

You can always find bags of grass clippings in any neighborhood—free. Till in as many as you can, and add about 100 pounds of dry manure (or other balanced natural fertilizer) per 1000 square feet. Peat moss is a good soil conditioner and can be added freely, but the large bale type, sphagnum, doesn't contain any nutrients to speak of. Grass clippings, shredded leaves, and other organic materials will do more for the soil, but they should be at least partially decomposed before seeding time. A liquid natural fertilizer applied after tilling will speed up decomposition and preserve soil nitrogen.

REPLACING AN EXISTING LAWN

If you are planting a lawn where an old one exists, you have to decide whether to strip off the old lawn or turn it under. A heavy-duty rototiller can break up the old lawn and mix it deeply into the soil, providing a lot of otherwise lost organic matter.

The usual procedure is to kill off any undesirable weeds or grasses first, to lessen their chance of growing again after seeding is done. The most common method of killing off a lawn is by spraying it with an all-purpose vegetation killer. Glyphosate (also known as Round-up, Kleen-up, and Shootout) has been used primarily over the past decade, but I recently received news of a *naturally made* vegetation killer produced by Safer (known primarily for their natural insecticidal soaps). This will be available in spring 1988, and is going to be a tremendous advance for chemical-free landscaping.

It is also possible to kill off growth by continual short cutting (as low as possible), or by covering the area with black plastic or other opaque material to block the sunlight for a few weeks. When you till in the sod, mix in your fertilizer, lime, and other organic matter at the same time so it is distributed evenly and deeply. Add additional topsoil at this time if you want to raise the height of the lawn.

If you choose to strip the lawn off instead of going through all the labor involved with tilling it up, you'll need to rent a sod cutter. This machine makes quick work of the old lawn, peeling it off in strips about 1½ feet wide.

Next you'll have to add your soil amendments, and more topsoil if it's needed. Then till everything. The soil will be fluffed up, so don't be scared if it looks too high. It will settle some, and you'll be rolling it later, too.

After rototilling, there will be mounds and dips that you must level out. If the rototilling didn't give you a backache, this next job will. You'll get fast results with a three- or four-foot-wide grading rake, leveling first in one direction and then the other. You can get very inventive if you don't want to rent a grading rake. I've seen people drag the soil with heavy boards, pieces of chain link fence, wood ladders, and old bedsprings. All of these will work to scrape the high spots into the low ones. You can stretch a piece of string across the planting bed to determine your progress.

WAIT BEFORE SEEDING

The next step is to **give the ground a thorough soaking.** If you have the time, keep it watered for three or more weeks. Because August is too hot and dry for seeding, it's an excellent month for this step. The purpose of the watering is to settle the soil and to encourage weeds to sprout *before* you seed. You can pull them, hoe every few days, or even run a tiller over them (1–2 inches deep at most). The soil should not be tilled too finely. Larger bits of soil provide spots for the seed to settle in. Pulverized soil has no structure left to it and will crust up fast after getting wet. This crust can cause problems when watering, especially if the lawn is sloped. Level the soil again if you've disturbed it much during this step, or if the soil has settled unevenly. You might fertilize the top inch again now with starter fertilizer or something high in phosphorous to make sure the young seedlings have nutrients near them when they begin to grow.

Measure the area you are seeding to get a good idea of how many pounds of seed you need (according to the package's directions—most seed packages have spreader settings on them). The best way to put the seed down is with a drop spreader. It will distribute evenly and not allow the wind to toss the seed around. Mix the seed up before filling the spreader, and be careful to leave an opening large enough to let the large as well as small seeds (such as bluegrass) pass through.

Now criss-cross the yard with the spreader, trying to distribute about 15–20 seeds per square inch. Be sure to overlap the tracks of the spreader with each pass. After the seed is down, rake it in an eighth- to a quarter-inch deep with an inverted spring leaf rake.

If you've seeded in early September, all you need to do now is water enough to keep the soil from drying out. It would be beneficial to spread a light coat of peat moss on top of the soil, to conserve moisture and prevent water run-off. Soak it down fast so it doesn't blow away, or make it slightly moist and crumbly before you toss it on (no thicker than a half-inch). If you seeded in mid-to-late spring, or during the summer, the soil will need a thicker coat of peat or a covering of straw to keep the hot sun from quickly drying it out. Any mulch will help stabilize the soil temperature. Plants respond favorably to steady temperatures and steady amounts of moisture, which is why grass sprouts much faster through a light mulch.

You can leave peat moss and finer mulches where they are; they'll soon vanish into the lawn. Rake out a straw mulch. Let the grass grow an inch higher than normal before cutting it, and keep it on the high side at least until mid-fall. Use a sharp mower blade and mow carefully. Remember that there are other seeds in the seed mix that will be sprouting soon, or are just starting out.

SPOT-SEEDING

Spot-seed when you need to reestablish small areas of lawn, such as thin or tire-damaged sections. The simplest way to spot-seed is first to pull out the weeds, and then to scratch up the soil with a heavy metal dirt rake or cultivating tool (if there is already some good grass growing, carefully work around it). Next, mix ⅓ sphagnum peat moss with ⅔ good garden soil to get it light and spongy. Add 1½ cups of balanced organic fertilizer per bushel of soil, making sure that whatever fertilizer you use has plenty of phosphorous (P) to stimulate root growth.

"Starter fertilizers" are meant to be used with seed or sod, and are high in phosphorous, so use one of these if you can. Spread this mixture over the bare spot until it is slightly higher than the soil level of the surrounding grass. If possible, gently mix it into the scratched-up original soil. This way there won't be extremely good soil sitting on top of bad soil.

Now sprinkle on your seed. **Use a seed type similar to the existing grass,** unless it was the wrong grass to begin with. Don't skimp: about 15–20 seeds per square inch is right. Bury the seed an eighth- to a quarter-inch into the soil. Dragging a spring rake with the tines inverted is a good way to work the seeds deeper without pulling them away. Now gently tamp the soil until it's level with the surrounding soil. Don't tamp hard enough to compact the soil, because you want water to soak in easily. I always throw some extra seed just to the outside of the spot-seeded area. This helps the new grass blend in better when it grows.

For deeper damage, such as tire ruts, tamp the soil mix more firmly before adding the last inch or two of soil. This way you won't sink into the ground when you walk on it later. If the ruts are quite deep and you want to conserve your mix, fill the bottom of the ruts with good soil and put the mix on top. On golf courses, where divots are a constant nuisance, some groundskeepers mix seed in with their soil/peat/fertilizer blend. They scoop this mixture into the divot, gently step on it, and that's that. Some seed is wasted this way because it gets planted too deep, but mixing everything together saves time, and therefore money. Perhaps you should make up a batch of spot-seeding mix, and keep it around to use as an occasional quick-fix.

10♦SOD LAWNS

The fastest and perhaps simplest way to put in a lawn or repair a bad spot is to use **sod,** which might be called pre-grown grass. It's usually grown on a specially prepared field and harvested after living through one winter. Then it is stripped out of the field and sold in rolls that cover about ten square feet each. Because sod is already growing, all you have to do is keep it growing until it roots and establishes itself in your yard.

IS SOD WORTH THE EXPENSE?

Many people have heard that putting down sod is much more expensive than seeding a lawn. But the long-term cost difference is a lot less than the original price discrepancy. The major factors are time and water. You can water a sod lawn daily (sometimes less often) and have it fairly well established in two to three weeks; a seeded lawn might take two to three weeks of daily watering just to germinate. For the next week or two after that the lawn must not be allowed to dry out, or the young sprouts will die. Sometimes you might have to water twice a day. After that, you'll still have to keep watering as needed until the grass is firmly established.

Few people have access to free water. And finding time to water daily, especially when you have to move the sprinkler around to cover larger areas, is not easy in this busy world. As long as we're looking at the pros and cons, I'll give you a chart to examine.

Prepare soil for sod the same way you would prepare it for a seed lawn. Initially, sod will grow in almost any soil—I've seen it grow right through a graveled parking lot into the soil below—but it won't survive long unless the soil is rich enough to support healthy lawn growth. The sod you buy has probably been vigorously and chemically fed and treated—its shallow root system and somewhat matted form will attest to that. A rich soil planting bed will help it survive in its new home.

The main idea is to get the sod's roots to dig into the soil as quickly as possible. A speedy rooting will prevent the grass from drying out, and will get it established before snows or droughts hit. **Soil moisture, as well as soil nutrients, will attract the roots downward.** If you water the sod lightly rather than keeping the soil beneath it moist, the roots will grow into the sod itself rather than into the soil.

Sod—Pros

- Gives an instant green covering
- Establishes itself quickly
- Can be installed any time during the growing season (midsummer installations do demand much more watering)
- Can be placed on slopes and not wash away with the rains
- Smothers many potential weeds that are near the soil surface

Sod—Cons

- Higher cost
- Very limited choice of grasses
- Sometimes is so tightly matted that it needs aerating for water and fertilizers to penetrate
- Might bring in insects, disease, or weeds

Seed—Pros

- Almost unlimited variety available to match yard conditions and owner preference
- Less expensive than sod
- Can be sown very fast over large areas, especially if the right equipment is available
- Will normally grow on its own at the right time with no further help from you after sowing the seed. Therefore, seed can be planted anytime and left alone (but grass won't grow until it is ready).

Seed—Cons

- Demands more time and water
- Has weed competition
- Hard to plant on slopes
- Can't be installed from late spring to midsummer with good results
- Will usually need spot-seeding for areas that don't fill in

You'll end up with instant thatch instead of instant lawn.

When you use sod to patch a small spot in your lawn, simply dig out an area about an inch deep (deeper for thicker southern sods), scratch up the soil (adding some starter fertilizer if you have it), and lay down the sod so that it fits in nicely and is level with the original lawn. Step softly on it, or roll it, until the sod comes in good contact with the soil. Soak it well enough to make sure the soil below is saturated, then water as needed to keep the sod and soil from drying out.

If you are putting in a complete sod lawn, make sure your soil is loaded with nutrients and organic matter to provide years of healthy growth. The soil should be firm to step on, but the top half-inch or so should be scratched up and sprinkled with starter fertilizer. Grade the soil away from the house and about an inch down wherever it meets walks or driveways. This will protect the sod's edges from exposure to drying wind and sun.

Sod should be laid out in a staggered pattern, similar to the way bricks are normally layered. The seams on the shorter side of the sod pieces should be close to the middle of the pieces above and below it. If the lawn has a slope to it, lay the sod across rather than down the slope. This will prevent water from forming channels in the seams during watering or heavy rains.

The typical home yard has a straight walkway or driveway to use as a border for your first strip. Unroll the sod along that starter strip first, then begin the next strip with a half piece of sod, so its end will line up with the middle of the first piece in your starter strip. Then continue on with full pieces. Keep the seams as tight as possible, but don't overlap them.

Never stretch the sod when you lay it down. It will shrink a little when it dries out and you'll find gaps between the seams. To cut off the ends of the sod strips, or to cut around trees or beds, use a long sharp knife or a sharp, straight-edged spade or edging tool. These pieces come in handy for replacing the bad sections of sod that inevitably turn up as you unroll it.

When you have finished laying down the sod, give the whole lawn a good rolling with a half full roller. This will ensure good contact with the soil, as well as tighter seams. After rolling, *gently* rake the top of the sod to straighten up the grass and make the seams less visible. Good sod that is cut in standard-size pieces makes for remarkably fast installation.

CHOOSING YOUR SOD

If you live anywhere near a large city, there are probably two or more growers to supply you or your local nurseries. The sod should be freshly harvested, moist, and green. If it has been sitting around for a long time, the blades will be high and the mat will be extremely tight due to continuous growth into itself. The mat of the sod should be about ¾–1¼ inches thick for bluegrass sod, thicker for St. Augustine (excluding blade height). Sod cut too thin will die very fast. Don't accept yellowish colored sod. It might merely have been kept rolled up for a few days, but it might also be infested.

The growers in my area sell only bluegrass-blend sod, which doesn't grow well in heavily shaded spots, so I don't always use it. Make sure that the sod you buy matches the environment you plan to use it in. You should always look over the sod carefully for discoloration of the leaf blades, which might signify disease. Check underneath for grubs or other lawn insects, and don't accept any sod that is infested.

In New York and some other states, sod can be "certified." This will guarantee that there are certain types of grasses in it, and will give you some, though not complete, assurance that it has been treated for insects and disease. **Once you have the sod at your property, do not let it dry out.** If it is rolled or folded, install it within forty-eight hours.

OTHER TIPS ON SOD

Always make sure to keep the sod that is against walks or driveways well watered. These places tend to dry out faster because of the water-absorbing qualities of concrete and similar paving materials. These materials also retain heat on sunny days, causing the soil in contact with them to dry out quickly.

When watering your new sod, remember not to walk on it if the ground is thoroughly saturated. You'll sink in and make a mess of your new lawn. If you need to move your sprinkler around to get the whole area wet, figure out a system that will let you move it without walking all over the soaked lawn.

Finally, as I mentioned earlier, please don't cut your sod lawn too short. Keep it at least three inches high if it is a bluegrass lawn. It will look tremendous at that height, and its roots will dig in fast and deep.

If you try to cut it short, you'll ruin it in one season. I've seen this happen many times. If you have read this far into the book, I think you know exactly why the sod should be cut long, and I'm sure you will keep it that way.

PLUGGING AND SPRIGGING

Perhaps you've seen the ads for zoysiagrass—the miracle grass you "plug" into your lawn. Most Northerners have no idea what plugs are—or sprigs, either. Here is a description of how they work.

Plugs

Plugs are simply small circles or squares of turf with a couple inches of soil attached. These "biscuits," as they are sometimes called, are first cut out of an existing lawn and then planted about 6–12 inches apart in the new lawn area. A special plugging tool can be used both to dig out plugs and make holes for the plugs to be set in. Once planted they're lightly rolled, watered well, and kept moist until they're established.

Plugging is usually reserved for the hearty stoloniferous grasses of the South, and occasionally used with strong rhizomatous grasses, too. It can be done on a freshly prepared lawn bed, or plugs can be set into an existing lawn either for repairs or for the end result of a new dominant grass type. Zoysiagrass, plugged at twelve inches apart on a bluegrass lawn, will completely crowd out the bluegrass in about four years.

Commercially produced plugs are usually sliced up in squares from pieces of sod. This saves waste. The plugs can be mechanically planted behind a tractor.

Sprigs

A sprig is simply a piece of stem—a stolon or rhizome—that has nodes (or joints) which are capable of rooting and forming individual new plants. You can purchase sprigs as individual pieces (by the bushel), or you can take sod (Bermudagrass, zoysia, St. Augustine) and pull it apart into individual sprigs. Always keep sprigs (and plugs) shaded and slightly moist while you're waiting to plant them. They have no soil on them and can dry out within minutes on a sunny or windy day.

Planting Sprigs

On a prepared lawn bed that has been soaked the previous day, dig out 2–3-inch furrows (channels) in straight lines 4–12 inches apart. Then set the sprigs in the furrows 6–12 inches from each other. Cover the sprigs, leaving a small portion (the greenest part) sticking up above ground. Roll lightly and irrigate. Take care not to let the sprigs dry out in the furrow before they're watered.

Stolonizing is another method of sprigging. The sprigs are broadcast over an area as evenly as possible, and then gently pushed into the soil by disking. Or the sprigs are covered over (topdressed) with a half inch of soil or fine mulch, and then rolled firmly. Whichever method you choose, plant only as much at one time as you can without letting the sprigs dry out.

Incidentally, you can topdress a lawn every couple of weeks with up to half an inch of fine soil brushed or raked off the blades and down to the base of the plant. Do this when you want to raise a low spot on the lawn. But don't put too much soil on at once, or the grass will be smothered.

SEED MATS

This is a fairly new product that shows great potential for both homeowner and commercial applications. Lightweight rolls of highly absorbent material are impregnated with grass seed and perhaps a starter fertilizer. The material is rolled out over soil that has been prepared for seeding, and then watered until fully saturated. The grass sprouts and roots into the soil underneath the mat. The weeds that typically sprout when grass is seeded won't penetrate through the mat and should die off. After a few months, however, the mat will decompose and there's nothing left but lawn.

Much of the advantage of using such products is their ease of handling. A 5′ × 50′ (250 square feet) roll weighs about as much as one moist roll of sod (10 square feet), and it goes down very fast, with no waste. No problems, such as insects or disease or thatch, can come in with it. Different seed blends can be put into the mats and unused material can be stored for later use. Look for seed mats to come on strong in the next decade.

11 ◆ LAWN CHEMICALS: AN OVERVIEW

The next three chapters deal with lawn problems that have in recent history been handled with chemicals. My advice, as you might expect, is to avoid using lawn chemicals if at all possible. Use the least toxic approach. You have every right to a nice lawn, but try to keep a balanced perspective. Lawns are not like food crops that must keep the world from starving; a few weeds or insects are not worth panicking about. Before applying pesticides (an all-inclusive term for insecticides, fungicides, herbicides, and rodenticides), you should understand the effects they *might* have on you, your family, and your community. Learn about the alternatives to pesticides and make an informed decision.° There are somewhere between thirty to fifty thousand pesticide formulations available today. Perhaps 10 percent of them have had some sort of safety assessment done on them. I used to believe that those deemed safe for the general public were fairly harmless. But as the years roll on new data keeps emerging, and as quick as a new product comes out, another is taken off the shelves. At this point I'm unwilling to say that any synthetic chemical pesticide is completely safe.

Lawn chemicals can enter your body in a variety of ways, most directly by skin contact and inhalation. Insecticides are particularly dangerous since most of them contain poisons similar to the ones in nerve gas. Common pesticide poisoning symptoms I've seen as a professional in the lawn business include headaches, runny noses, rashes, and nausea. My dog developed warts twenty-four hours after exposure to an insecticide. Other symptoms are vomiting, heavy sweating, dizziness, and disorientation. Dioxin, found in Dacthal and 2, 4-D (longtime "safe" choice for home lawn herbicides), has been shown to cause cancer in laboratory animals. Numerous other problems, affecting almost every organ of the body, have been connected with, or are suspected of being connected with, pesticide use. Testing is only in

°For more information on pesticides write NCAMP (National Coalition Against the Misuse of Pesticides), 530 7th Street S.E., Washington, DC 20003.

the infant stages. A wise doctor once told my mother that unless there were a life-and-death situation, he would never give her any drug that hadn't undergone at least twenty years of testing. Sound advice. Why not apply it to our lawn drugs?

A thick, healthy lawn and a living soil are your best protection against lawn problems, but what should you do in the meantime, while you're working at getting your lawn and soil really healthy? Or what if, despite your best efforts, your lawn contracts a serious illness?

Treat your lawn the same way you might treat your body if you didn't want to use drugs. If you had an upset stomach and you thought it might be something serious, you would go to a doctor and ask for his diagnosis. Then you would decide whether you knew how to handle the problem on your own (with diet, vitamins, herbs, or whatever), and whether your self-treatment might turn the problem around before it got worse. Finally, you would choose a treatment and proceed with it. I've avoided the use of medications for about thirteen years now, but if I did get seriously ill, and a natural cure wasn't immediately available, you can be sure that I would take whatever the doctor prescribed.

A similar situation arises when your lawn has a serious problem. As a landscaper I am often confronted with this dilemma, and sometimes I have to use chemicals. A client either doesn't want to wait for a slow cure, or a lawn is in such bad shape that if immediate action isn't taken, there will soon be no lawn left. Weigh your alternatives and find out what natural solutions are available. Visit the nurseries, not just the garden section of the local department store or supermarket, and see what they have to offer. Try to make an informed decision for which you can take full responsibility. But always remember to keep working at building that healthy lawn and soil so you'll avoid similar situations in the future.

The natural and biological lawn care products industry is still in its infancy, and that is quite encouraging. Great strides have already been made with miniscule amounts of funding. Credit must be given to J.I. Rodale, one of the foremost pioneers of organic gardening in America. And we also owe a debt of gratitude to Rachel Carson, whose book *Silent Spring* helped bring a higher sense of environmental awareness to this country.

Despite the fact that there is still plenty of research and development to be done, there are quite a few natural lawn care products on the market. Some of these are only available by mail-order, but most of the natural products catalogs are quite educational and worth reading. I've listed some sources in the back of the book, and I'm sure I'll hear about more of them from knowledgeable readers. Tell your friends and the salespeople at your garden center that you are using natural products and that you encourage them to do likewise. With more support, the natural lawn care products industry will develop faster. Once people have learned to care for their lawns naturally, they won't want to do it any other way.

LAWN DISEASES

The average rural lawn seldom has problems with lawn disease. I don't see much of it on unsprayed suburban lawns, either. It isn't that disease and fungus are not in the soil and air in these places—they're around just as much as cold germs are. Disease in a lawn is just an indicator of poor lawn and soil health.

We already know that a weak lawn is more likely to be hurt by disease, so it makes sense to keep our lawns as healthy as possible. But it is also true that a living soil contains a wholesome assortment of microbes that will control or prevent disease. Anything that kills soil life makes a lawn more prone to disease. Is it any wonder that lawns treated with too much chemical fertilizer need frequent spraying? And, of course, the chemical disease-controlling sprays kill off even more soil life.

To illustrate this point a little more clearly, we can make an analogy between soil health and human health. Consider the parents of an infant who has a common ear infection. The doctor prescribes an antibiotic. The ear infection gets better, but the child gets diarrhea because the antibiotic has not only killed the offending microorganisms in the ear, but the valuable intestinal microorganisms known as flora. Antibiotics, like agricultural chemicals, don't distinguish between helpful and harmful microorganisms. Too much of a chemical that is meant to kill lawn fungus or harmful insects might destroy much of the life that your soil needs to stay healthy.

Thatch, as mentioned in a previous chapter, is a wonderful breeding ground for disease. The same things that cause thatch will cause disease: poor soil structure, bad watering and mowing habits, lifeless soil, and overuse of chemicals. The only permanent solution is to bring your lawn into a healthy condition and then keep it that way.

IS IT A DISEASE?

Diagnosing lawn diseases can be a little tricky. Not all of them stick out like mushrooms. (Mushrooms, by the way, are the fruits of fungus caused by rotting wood in the soil, usually from past construction or old tree roots and stumps. They cause the grass no real harm, and should be picked, raked, or mowed away if they bother you. There is no chemical that will prevent them.) Sometimes insect damage or chemicals create conditions that look like disease, but are not. Usually you'll see patches or spots of brown grass, or grass blades wilted or coated with some type of growth. This is a good time to consult a lawn doctor: a trained turf care professional. Some of the lawn spraying companies train their employees to diagnose lawn diseases. Your county extension agent could help. Once a knowledgeable professional has identified the problem, it is up to you to decide how to handle it. Sometimes a good dose of soapy water is all that's needed. There are also quite a few natural disease controls you can purchase by mail.

The recommendations you get from most spraying companies will be along the chemical lines. Check first to see if soap and water won't do the trick. Or perhaps one of the natural products on the market will take care of the problem. If the disease is caused by thatch, overly wet soil, compaction, or incorrect pH, you can correct these problems without a direct attack on the disease organism—which is, after all, only a symptom.

Ask yourself how critical the situation is and how fast you need results. Often, by the time the disease is noticed and identified, the damage has already been done. The climate has changed and the disease is no longer active. A chemical won't have any benefit if this is the case.

If you decide that chemical spraying is absolutely necessary, I suggest that you contract a professional to do it. The right materials, equipment, and techniques can make a big difference in the job's effectiveness. You will also avoid contact with the chemicals. Once the spraying is finished, do everything possible to eliminate the conditions that caused the disease.

NATURAL DISEASE PREVENTION

Aside from building the health of your soil and lawn, there are some specific ways to prevent lawn disease.

1. Most important, **plant a mixture of grasses rather than just a single variety.** Diseases can be quite selective, and a mixture of grasses will prevent complete destruction of your lawn.

2. Plant disease-resistant varieties. Check with your nursery person or the Lawn Institute on this one.

3. Make sure you aren't over-watering. If you can't keep your lawn surface-dry, consider drain tile or regrading. Disease is not a problem in arid regions of the country.

4. Water sufficiently. Under-watering a lawn, to keep it barely growing when it should either be heavily watered or allowed to go dormant, will also lead to weak, disease- and insect-prone grass.

5. Make sure there is a free flow of air. Thin out dense shrub or tree growth to open up the yard a little.

6. Remove thatch. It creates a humid jungle on top of the soil and helps disease proliferate. **Aerating** breaks through thatch and reduces soil compaction.

7. Try a soap spray occasionally. Lawns that haven't been treated naturally for very long can benefit from a soap treatment. It breaks up the static and adherence above and below the soil for a short time and allows air and water to penetrate. The soap itself is antagonistic to disease organisms. A couple of cups of biodegradable dish soap in a 15-20 gallon hose-end sprayer is fine. Or do what Jerry Baker, America's Master Gardener, does. He was taught by an old-time greens-keeper to cut up a bar of Fels Naptha soap and dissolve it in hot water and make a spray out of it. That kept the greens and approaches disease-free.

Think about using some of the sea products and special fertilizers that have supplemental microbes and enzymes. It's tough for disease to get started with all that life in the soil. Ringer Research sells a fertilizer called Lawn Restore that has proved very effective against two common lawn diseases—fusarium and yellow patch. Let me quote Ringer Research's information sheet:

> Lawn Restore does not kill lawn diseases. It creates a soil environment conducive to luxuriant

growth. Three years of testing at a top turf university in the United States have proven that Lawn Restore eliminates conditions that cause lawn diseases. Fusarium and yellow patch are caused by lack of soil microorganisms and insufficient amounts of organic materials. Lawn Restore replenishes the soil with these important ingredients. The soil is revitalized and able to combat disease.

This is fascinating. Products like Lawn Restore can fertilize and prevent disease at the same time. And we are talking about long-lasting effects, not ones gone with the first rain. Did I mention that thatch is also reduced through the use of these living fertilizers? Not surprising. The chemical solution to lawn disease is to kill off soil life without discrimination. The natural solution is to add life to the soil. To organic gardeners, this idea is old hat. But to the majority of the world, this is a completely new approach to lawn care.

12 ♦ INSECTS IN THE LAWN

Healthy soils and lawns are teeming with insect life. Most insects are harmless, some are beneficial, and some are harmful to a lawn. In nature, healthy plants are not the first to be attacked by insects and disease. The weak and damaged get hit first. Tests have shown insects crawling over healthy fields to reach weaker plants. Once again, it appears that our basic solution to any lawn problem—create a healthy lawn and soil—is the answer to potential insect infestation.

HOW TO BRING ON THE INSECTS

If you do want to attract insects to your lawn, here's how you can do it. Cut the grass short so it stays constantly weak. Fertilize with quick-release chemicals that force soft topgrowth to develop without equal root growth to support it. Water lightly and often. Keep the top of the soil wet, but allow the root area to dry up. Don't do anything about thatch, or you might remove the insects' home. Make sure you kill off all soil life so the lawn develops complete chemical dependency. You'll have all the insects you could ever want.

Seriously, if you should have an insect problem, follow the same procedure as you would for lawn disease. First ask someone who knows insects to identify the offending animal. Then you can consider the various ways to eliminate or control it. Determine how quickly action must be taken, and weigh the consequences of anything you might choose to do. A few years ago I wouldn't have been able to recommend much for the homeowner in the way of natural controls, but things are improving rapidly. There are dozens of products on the market that are made to prevent insects, destroy them, or both. For instance, the Attack brand biological controls put out by Reuter Labs can now be found in most quality garden centers. As a rule, individual stores don't carry the entire line of a company's products, so if you find a product that looks promising, just write for the catalog of the company that sells it.

COMMON LAWN INSECTS

Grubs

By far the most damaging insect I've ever seen in a lawn is the white grub, which is actually the infant form of many types of beetles. When the beetles (Japanese beetle, June beetle, May beetle, chafers) feed on weak shrubs and trees, they lay eggs in nearby attractive (to them) lawns. The eggs hatch and the larval form of the beetle, called the grub, is born.

Grub.

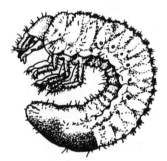

The white grub is a C-shaped, grey-white worm, about an inch long. Its small head is gray-brown.

Grubs destroy grass by chewing the roots off. They move slowly across the lawn, completely killing each grass plant in their path. If you see a dead or dying area of a grub-infested lawn and grab the grass in your hand, it will pull up like a carpet; there are no roots holding the turf down anymore. To make matters worse, moles and skunks in search of the tasty grubs can tear up a lawn overnight. This is one insect that I try to eliminate as fast as possible if it is doing noticeable damage. Having a few grubs here and there is not unusual. But when you have a real infestation you must act fast.

Sometimes you can get a jump on grubs precisely because they are such tasty food for larger animals. If you see flocks of birds on your lawn pecking away, or little holes all over indicating that birds were digging, check for grubs. If you notice any digging from a skunk, or the raised tunnel of a mole, check for grubs. Most people don't realize that you can often get rid of skunks and moles by getting rid of grubs. These animals wouldn't be digging up your lawn unless there was something to eat. Without these larger animals appearing on your lawn, there's a good possibility you wouldn't look for grubs until a good-size portion of your lawn had been ruined. So don't curse the animals. They are only indicators—advanced warning signals.

Mole Repellent

Try making an emulsion of two parts castor oil and one part liquid detergent in the blender. Add an equal amount of water, then put two tablespoons of the solution in a sprinkling can of water and pour it over the area where the moles are at work.

If you spot the grubs in time, you can try using a biological control on them. One of the newer controls is a beneficial parasitic nematode (a tiny soil insect), currently marketed as Scanmask, that feeds on over 230 harmful soil pests. I haven't tried it yet, but the literature I've received on it from Natural Garden Research Center's retail catalog makes good sense. The nematodes act quickly, and they don't harm any beneficial insects or earthworms. They will also handle many insects in vegetable gardens, trees, and houseplants.

One product I have tried is called milky spore powder, or *Bacillus popilliae*. It is a sure control for Japanese beetle grubs, as well as a few other lawn-eating grubs. Commercially known as Grub Attack, it is a long-lasting prevention that multiplies quickly and can stay dormant for years. The actual organism is a bacterial spore that gets eaten by the grub. The spores multiply like mad in the grub's body, killing the grub and then releasing billions of new spores into the soil. You should get fifteen to twenty years of grub control from one application, less if the grub population is completely wiped out and no new eggs are deposited. Some researchers say Grub Attack isn't effective in very cold areas, but I used it in the Syracuse, New York area, which is snowbelt country, and saw no beetles for three years after I applied it. Your county extension agent should be able to tell you how effective milky spore powder will be on the grub types in your area.

Another natural control is diatomaceous earth. This is a fine, razor-sharp dust that is made from the fossilized skeletons of a class of algae. Insects ingest it or slice their soft bodies on it. Either way, they die. Earthworms can digest it without harm. Spread 15–20 pounds per 1000 square feet of lawn up to four times a year. Mix some soap powder with it for an even more lethal solution.

Sod Webworms

Another frequent lawn pest is the sod webworm. If you have lots of moths flying in jerky patterns over the lawn, they are probably adult webworms. They lay their eggs in the grass, then hatch into small caterpillars that chew off the grass (above the thatch line, if there is thatch) and pull it into silky tunnels to eat it. You'll see small dead spots on the lawn by late spring, which may join up into larger spots as the summer progresses. The caterpillars feed at night, and are visible under a flashlight. Or you can watch them crawl to the surface if you pour a gallon of soapy water on the lawn. Birds on the lawn might indicate sod webworms.

Sod webworm.

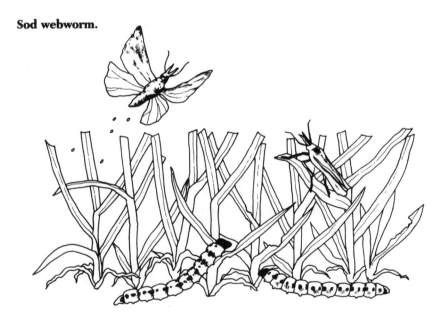

There are a few natural controls for caterpillar-type lawn pests. Scanmask, the parasitic nematode discussed above, lists sod webworm under its susceptible pests.

A few companies market B.t. (*Bacillus thuringiensis*), which is essentially a natural caterpillar-killing bacteria. If you had sod webworms the previous year, apply it early. Most biological pesticides work best on the larval stage of an insect. Again, try soap and water every couple of weeks. Safer's insecticidal soap, made from naturally occurring fatty acids, is a little better (and more expensive) than most dish soaps and is available in most garden centers.

Chinch Bugs

Chinch bugs are common in lawns both North and South. They love thatch, and are St. Augustinegrass's greatest enemy. If you pushed a bottomless coffee can a few inches into the soil of an infested lawn and then filled it with water, chinch bugs would float up.

Fight chinch bugs by fighting thatch. You can try diatomaceous earth and Scanmask, too. However, soap and water every ten to fourteen days will also do the trick. Jerry Baker suggests 50 pounds of gypsum per 2500 square feet.

Many other insects might feed on your lawn, but I won't attempt to discuss all of them here. The lawn professionals, books, and charts at your nursery or garden center will help you identify them.

A look at the Safer and Reuter Labs catalogs show that natural controls already exist for the following potential invaders of lawns: aphids, mites, sod webworms, grubs (some types), fleas, wasps, ants, mosquitos, and grasshoppers. Add diatomaceous earth and homemade soap sprays to this list, and we've got most of our insect problems covered.

I want you to keep in mind that a truly healthy lawn, as described in this book, will not be attractive to most insects. If you view insects as *symptoms* of an unhealthy lawn, you'll have greater long-term success getting rid of them. While you are working at building a healthy lawn you can keep most insect problems under control by using natural methods and natural products. It takes a little more effort and involvement with your lawn than simply spraying chemical insecticides, but I believe it is worth the trouble.

CHEMICAL CONTROLS

If you feel the use of chemical insecticides is justified in your particular case, you should know how to choose the one the Environmental Protection Agency feels is least toxic for the job. The E.P.A. doesn't allow pesticides to be on the shelves if they don't feel they are safe to use as directed. But they do rate pesticides (and many common household products) as to their degree of toxicity to the applicator. One of the following code words will appear on the label: DANGER–most lethal; WARNING–less lethal; and CAUTION–slightly lethal. They also make sure the label tells you if the product is known to be highly toxic to fish, birds, or other wildlife.

History has shown that no pesticide should be considered completely safe in the long run. So if you must use one, remember the following rules:

1. **Never allow insecticides to touch your skin.**
2. **Avoid inhalation.**
3. **If the insecticide is meant to be watered into the soil, do so immediately, before birds or other wildlife can come into contact with it.**
4. **Don't apply insecticide to lawns that might allow run-off or leaching into a stream, pond, or other aquatic environment.**

Handle natural pesticides with the same care as you would chemical pesticides. Don't take chances—a poison is a poison. Many chemical pesticides are imitations of substances found in nature. A little hemlock juice was all it took to kill Socrates, right?

The pesticide applicator finds himself in a position similar to the pharmacist's. He hopes all the products he deals with have been tested sufficiently and proven safe. He wants to provide a valuable service to his community. He doesn't want to find out in twenty years that some of his "medicines" have turned out to be as damaging to future generations as the drug D.E.S. But any supposedly safe drug or chemical poses certain risks in the long run. Most of the pesticide applicators today use the safest products that they feel will do the job. Don't think for a minute that they aren't concerned with their health or the health of others. It won't be hard to convince these people to use natural products once they have been shown to be effective and economical.

If you evaluate your situation and determine that pesticides are the answer to your problem, then try to use them only once. After that has been done, be sure to double your efforts to turn your lawn into a living picture of health. You won't have to worry about insects once that is achieved.

13♦WEED CONTROL

We now come to the third lawn problem that has commonly been treated with chemicals as a sole solution. Weeds are an especially challenging problem because some of them love the same soil conditions that grass thrives in. Nature intends the soil surface to be covered with plant growth. If grass isn't there, weeds will be soon. For almost twelve years now I've heard how each homeowner's weeds came from the neighbor's lawn. It's more accurate to say that weeds are there because a thick healthy lawn isn't!

If I were to say that you could rid your lawn of all weeds without chemicals or hand pulling, I would be dreaming. But you can change certain lawn conditions, improve your mowing, watering, and fertilizing habits enough to make your lawn unacceptable to most weeds. Your lawn can reach the point at which chemical weed killers aren't needed.

In case you are wondering, there are no natural products that can be spread over the whole lawn and kill only weeds. However, individual weeds or grasses can be spot-killed by a natural vegetation killer that was introduced while this book was in the editor's hands. This is a major advancement. As mentioned earlier, research has shown that some grass types, as well as other kinds of vegetation, release their own chemicals that inhibit or kill neighboring plants of a different variety. Strains of grass could be developed that would utilize this attribute to the homeowner's advantage. Considering the speed at which research is progressing toward natural solutions, I wouldn't be surprised to see a natural herbicide within the next few years that could be spread over the entire lawn without damaging the grass.

Leaving a few weeds scattered about your lawn is not a crime. Weeds are simply *unwanted* plants on a given piece of land. Orchids could start growing in your lawn and they would technically be weeds if they hadn't been planted there. It just so happens that the air and soil are loaded with seeds of plants that you don't want in your lawn. There are reasons why some of these sprout and grow, and these

120

reasons are what you are going to learn about in this chapter. Fortunately, most of the factors that discourage weeds make for better lawn growth.

UNDERSTANDING WEEDS

Weeds can be classified as **narrowleaf** (grassy) weeds or **broadleaf** weeds. A narrowleaf weed is often an undesirable type of grass that is in your lawn. Or it might be a plant that looks similar to grass in many ways. It doesn't blend with the rest of your lawn in color, thickness, height, or growing habits. Rough-bladed tall fescue, mentioned earlier, is usually considered a grassy weed in otherwise fine-bladed lawns.

Broadleaf weeds are exactly what they sound like. They can have large, small, wide, pointed, rounded, or thick leaves. They don't look like grass at all. The dandelion, with its yellow flower, is our most common broadleaf weed.

Weeds are usually either **annuals** or **perennials.** Annuals grow one season, drop their seeds, and die. Perennials grow year after year, even if their tops disappear over the winter. Most of them go to seed at least once during each growing season.

Finally, you must understand that although many weeds thrive in the same soil conditions that lawns require, many others will grow only in poor conditions. Some like it wet, some dry. Some like acid, some alkaline. Some need sun, some want shade. By creating a healthy lawn and soil, you will be uncreating the conditions that many weeds enjoy. This is a unique approach to weed control, similar to the approach we use toward insects and disease.

CONTROLLING WEEDS

The first step toward eradicating your weeds is to identify them. I've included some drawing, but a nursery keeper or lawn pro would be of better help. You can pull up a weed and carry it to an expert for identification.

Once you have identified a weed, don't go right for the chemicals. I'm going to provide as much information as I can to help you understand why that weed is there, and what you can do to discourage it. Weeds do have some use. They can, by their presence alone, tell you what is wrong with your soil or lawn care practices. If you choose to use a chemical, I suggest spot-killing the individual plants so you don't have to put the chemical on the weed-free portion of the lawn. I'll talk more about this later.

HERBICIDES

There are several types of herbicides that are normally applied. **Pre-emergent** herbicides are spread on the lawn before certain weeds sprout. They create a film on the soil and are usually used to kill annual grassy weeds as they germinate—that is, before they have emerged through the soil surface. **Post-emergent** herbicides are applied directly to weeds that are already up and growing. These are mostly used to control specific broadleaf weeds. They don't kill other weeds or grasses. Most lawn post-emergents today are **systemic,** which means they are absorbed into the system of the plant and kill the whole thing. **Contact** herbicides, on the other hand, are post-emergents that only kill the tops of plants. They are not effective on thick-rooted weeds like dandelions. **Non-selective** herbicides will kill any vegetation they are applied to, lawn grass included. They are normally used on perennial narrowleaf weeds or undesirable lawn grasses when nothing else will work. Safer's new, non-selective weed and grass killer is the first natural herbicide to hit the market. The fact sheet says it's made from a blend of fatty acids that are biodegradable and non-toxic to people and pets. It works extremely fast and allows reseeding of the lawn after forty-eight hours. I can't wait to try it this spring.

Most over-the-counter herbicides claim to be biodegradable when used correctly. Some are more like hormones than straight poisons. Still, even with the "safest" of the weedkillers, there is the possibility of toxic reaction from skin exposure or inhalation before they have had a chance to break down. Also, post-emergent herbicides are supposed to kill weeds selectively and not harm the grass. But under the right conditions of stress on the lawn, herbicides *will* damage the grass. In fact, a post-emergent herbicide applied on the grass in such a situation becomes an additional stress factor that could destroy the lawn. I know I'm being redundant, but play it safe with any lawn chemical. Use it wisely, only when needed, and then try to change lawn conditions so you won't need it again.

INDIVIDUAL WEEDS AND THEIR CONTROLS

I couldn't include every lawn weed in a book of this nature. There are many I haven't listed that will compete with your lawn. If you can't identify a weed, bring it to your local nursery and have it checked against charts or books for that particular weed's habits. Then make your own decision about how to handle it.

Annual bluegrass (*Poa annua*). An annual mostly, but there are some perennial and biennial species (biennials go to seed and then die in their second year of growth). Annual bluegrass sprouts early and may go to seed by late spring. It sprouts again and seeds in fall. It likes cool and moist conditions, and will wilt severely in midsummer, opening up space for other weeds to grow in. Shallow-rooted. Hand pull and correct the soil. Pre-emergent chemical control.

Bermudagrass (devilgrass). In more southern areas, Bermudagrass is your best lawn choice. In transition areas, where you want a cool-season grass to grow, Bermudagrass becomes an invasive weed. It is a narrowleaf perennial that grows best in the heat and sun (where cool-season grasses fare worst), but it takes on a dormant brown color in the fall as the cool-season grasses recover. A non-selective vegetation killer is needed to eliminate it.

Broad-leaved plantain and **Narrow-leaved plantain.** These perennials are often called crabgrass by those who don't know better. Both are actually broadleaf weeds. They fill in bare areas and establish from seed rather quickly on thin lawns. Hand pull them, or use a post-emergent chemical. Thicken-up your lawn.

Cinquefoil. A broadleaf perennial, cinquefoil has leaves that look like strawberry leaves. It indicates acid, infertile, and sandy soil. You can easily control it with a thick turf on a good soil, or with a post-emergent.

Common chickweed. This broadleaf annual prefers cool, moist weather and shade, as well as slightly acid soils. It grows poorly in summer heat. **Mouse-ear chickweed** is a perennial that withstands summer heat. It forms a fairly dense mat. Both weeds are chemically controlled by post-emergents.

Annual bluegrass.

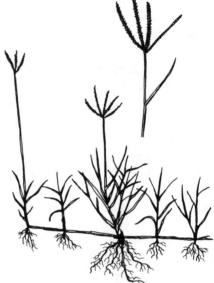

Bermudagrass.

Broad-leaved plantain.

Narrow-leaved plantain.

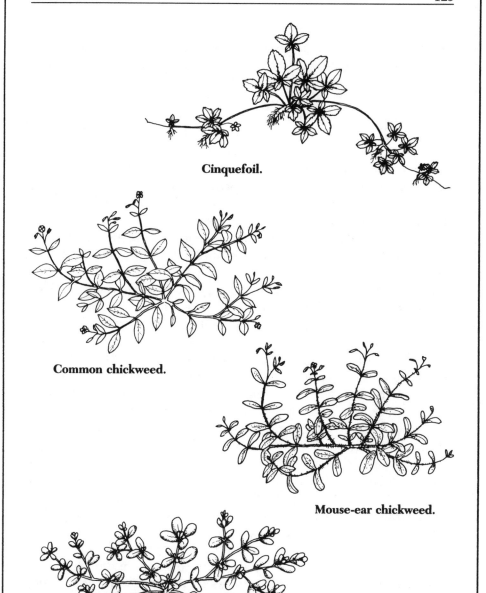

Cinquefoil.

Common chickweed.

Mouse-ear chickweed.

Common purslane.

Common purslane. Thick, fleshy leaves make this annual broad-leaf look like a prostrate-growing jade plant. It invades thin or new lawns, and can withstand hot and dry conditions. Control purslane with post-emergents, or simply thicken-up the lawn fast.

Crabgrass. For some reason, most novices to lawn care call most every weed they see "crabgrass." So let's clarify what it is right away. Crabgrass is a grassy weed, and an annual. The seeds dropped the previous summer will sprout to form new plants in the late spring, when the ground has completely warmed up. It has a low-growing, prostrate habit, shallow but strong roots, and it can't stand the shade. In the fall it turns brownish red and dies.

Crabgrass will invade close-cropped lawns, and lawns that are thin and have bare spots. The key to controlling it is to prevent it from getting the light it needs for good growth. Because it won't sprout until late spring when the soil is thoroughly warm, you can get a thick, high-cut lawn established long before the crabgrass sprouts. The shade of the thick, tall grass alone will prevent most of these sun-loving weeds from either sprouting or growing.

In the North, if you fertilize in midsummer you'll be fertilizing the crabgrass and other weeds, because cool-season grasses are probably dormant or near dormant at this time. Shallow watering is ideal for crabgrass, but deep watering, after allowing the top of the soil to dry out a bit, will discourage crabgrass. If you do get some in your lawn, try to pull it before the seeds drop.

Crabgrass and some of the other annual narrowleaf weeds are usually chemically treated by pre-emergent weed killers, which kill seeds in the soil as they sprout. Most of the pre-emergents also kill grass seeds, so read the package carefully if you plan to seed a lawn within two months of applying a pre-emergent.

A lawn that was heavily infested with crabgrass the previous season will be loaded with crabgrass seeds, ready to sprout in the late spring. The typical procedure would be to reseed the lawn while at the same time treating it with a safe-for-grass-seed pre-emergent (Siduron, Tupersan). There are no natural pre-emergents yet.

Once the lawn is good and thick, keep it high and you won't be bothered much by crabgrass. If some does pop up, you'll notice pale green tufts of it, which you should hand pull as soon as possible. Post-emergents are available for crabgrass, but they require two or

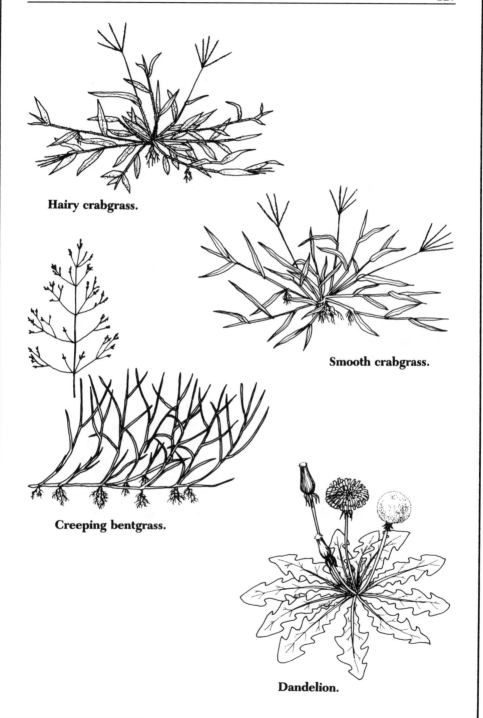

Hairy crabgrass.

Smooth crabgrass.

Creeping bentgrass.

Dandelion.

three applications, timed correctly. Even then, the results are not usually satisfactory.

Creeping bentgrass is a perennial, fine-bladed, horizontal-growing grass that acts like a weed when patches of it establish themselves in an upright lawn. Often you'll notice what appear to be dead, flat spots on the lawn after the snow melts. These are patches of bentgrass waiting for the soil to warm up.

You may also notice bentgrass when you rake your lawn and find very long blades or runners growing sideways. In an upright lawn, bentgrass will often look brown right after the lawn has been mowed, because only the very tops of the blades stay green.

Bentgrass is shallow-rooted and invades lawns that are constantly damp in the summertime. Since it tolerates short mowing while other grasses don't, it can quickly take over if you keep your lawn too short.

Bentgrass can be partially eliminated by keeping the soil surface dry most of the time, and keeping the bentgrass raked straight up so it doesn't spread through the lawn, re-rooting along the way. It can sometimes be controlled by strong post-emergent herbicides, but more often than not you'll have to use a non-selective herbicide to get rid of it.

Dandelion. This is the one with the beautiful yellow flowers that soon turn into white seed puffs that float in the wind. It has been used for greens, wine, and coffee, but for most of us it's just a weed in the lawn. A perennial, broadleaf weed, it develops a long, thick root which provides some benefit by breaking into the hard subsoil.

Dandelions become a problem in lawns that are too thin or cut too short. The seeds find their way to the soil and germinate easily. Once again, the best prevention is a thick, healthy lawn. It won't choke out seedlings; rather, it prevents their sprouting.

If you do have a few dandelions, spot-spray the individual plants with a non-selective, systemic herbicide (try the new natural product from Safer), or you can try to dig them out by hand. You'll develop a touch for this operation after a while; the young plants are easiest. Try not to snap the root, or you can expect it to grow again and maybe divide into two plants. Those thick roots store a lot of food, so keep after them even if you can't get the whole root. Eventually the roots will run out of food and die. Let the neighborhood kids or grandchildren earn some extra money by paying them a penny for each dandelion flower they pick. This will keep the dandelions from going to seed and blowing throughout the neighborhood. If you should see a white seed ball on a stem, carefully pick it off so the seeds don't blow away.

If there are too many dandelions for hand weeding or spot-spraying, you'll have to bring them under control using a systemic post-emergent herbicide that gets the root and all.

Ground ivy and **Lawn pennywort.** Ground ivy has larger leaves, a mint smell, and purple flowers. Both plants are broadleaf perennials, creep on the soil surface, and send out roots. They prefer a damp soil surface. Control them with post-emergents or hand pulling, or improve the soil and lessen surface moisture.

Knotweed. Also called wine grass, knotweed is a broadleaf annual that can form a thick mat. It constantly reseeds itself, especially in compacted, infertile soils. Pull it when the soil is wet, then loosen the soil with organic matter and aerate. Knotweed can be treated with post-emergents.

Nimblewill (*Muhlenbergia*). This is a perennial, grassy, shallow-rooted weed. It likes a wet soil surface and a low-cut lawn. Hand pull it, or use a post-emergent.

Nut sedge and **dallisgrass.** These are perennials with light green, wide-bladed leaves; they indicate poor soil drainage. You can hand pull them, but you must correct the soil to get rid of them entirely. Post-emergent chemical control.

Oxalis (wood-sorrel). A perennial, broadleaf plant that kids chew on for its lemon taste. Its leaves look something like clover. Oxalis grows in hard, compacted soils. Improve soil conditions or use a post-emergent to get rid of it.

Spotted Spurge. An annual broadleaf that tolerates fertile or infertile soil. It germinates in late spring and early summer in thin and bare areas of the lawn. You can treat it with pre-emergent or post-emergent chemicals, but it is easy to hand pull when the soil is wet.

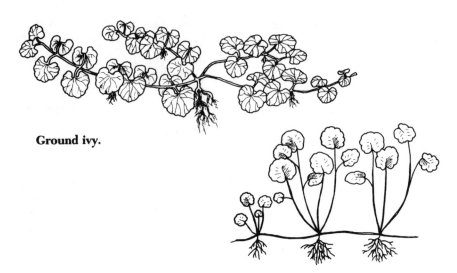

Ground ivy.

Lawn pennywort.

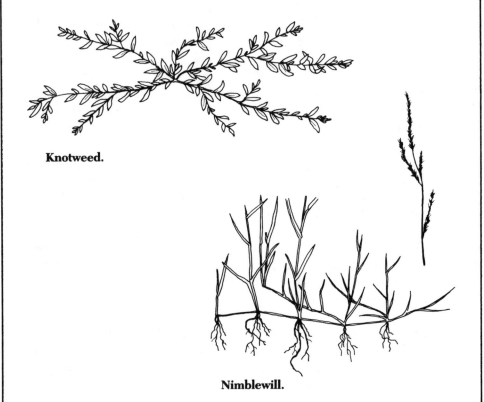

Knotweed.

Nimblewill.

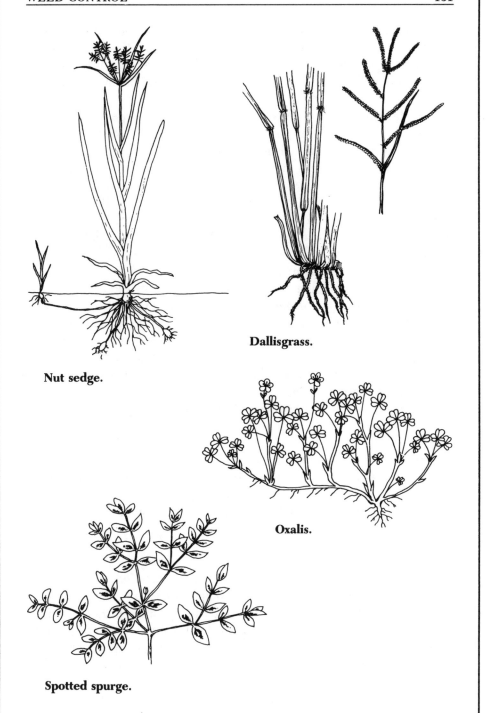

Nut sedge.

Dallisgrass.

Oxalis.

Spotted spurge.

Tall fescue is a coarse perennial grass that is considered a weed when it is not desired in a lawn. It grows in clumps that can get larger and larger. When the rest of your lawn is dormant or near dormant, tall fescue, with its wide, dull blades will stick out like a sore thumb.

Tall fescue is a lawn grass, even if it isn't the type you desire. It favors conditions similar to those the fine-bladed grasses thrive in. The best way to prevent it is to keep your lawn thick. If some does get in your lawn, you should dig it out. Pull all the blades to the center of the clump so you can see how wide the base actually is. Then dig it out by the roots, using a hand trowel or weeding tool. Patch the bare spot with seed or sod. If you feel too lazy to do this, you can occasionally slice into the center of the clump with a flat shovel or some such tool. This will weaken the plant and it might die off.

Tall fescue is not impressed by chemical weedkillers. Only a non-selective vegetation killer will have any effect on it, and if you sprayed such a substance on the fescue, it would also poison the good grass surrounding it. You can try dabbing the tips of the tall fescue with a paint brush (the sponge type, preferably) dipped in a non-selective vegetation killer during a time when the fescue is sticking out above the rest of the lawn. That would keep the rest of your lawn safe. Many people have learned to live with this grass when it's interspersed with taller grass types and not growing in unsightly clumps.

Veronica (thyme-leaved speedwell). There are perennial and annual varieties of this broad-leaved, spreading weed. It is similar to heal-all, another creeping broad-leaved perennial. A thick turf will keep both of them out, but if they are already established they must be handled with a post-emergent.

White clover. Grass seed mixes formerly included this broadleaf perennial. Its nitrogen-fixing activity helps to fertilize the grass around it, but its white flowers and bee-attracting qualities make it undesirable to some. Most post-emergents will control it whether you want it gone or not. The owner of Chem-Free lawn service says he eliminates it by cutting the lawn high, and then adding extra nitrogen around the clover.

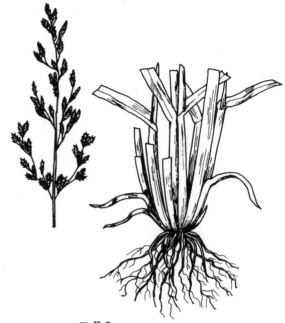

Tall fescue.

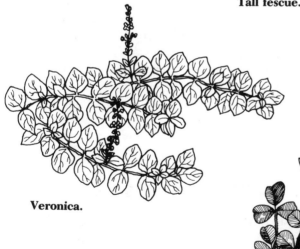

Veronica.

White clover.

MOSS AND ALGAE

These could also be listed under lawn diseases. They are lower forms of plant life that don't harm grass plants the way diseases do. They fill in weak areas and keep grass from growing there later.

Moss and algae might indicate poor soil structure, compacted soil, acid soil, and wet conditions. Moss shows up on infertile soils, but algae likes high fertility plus very high soil moisture. Liming sometimes helps alleviate moss and algae because of its ability to condition the soil into a better structure and to neutralize an acid soil. Any efforts toward aeration of the soil, increasing humus content, or bettering the soil structure to provide proper drainage, will help rid your lawn of both moss and algae. Reducing shade and increasing air flow will sometimes be enough. Extra fertilizer helps get rid of moss.

ABOUT THE SOUTH

Because the warm-season grasses of the South grow so vigorously in the hot summer, most lawn weeds appear in the late fall, winter, and early spring. Instead of just spraying all the weeds that would take over while the Bermudagrass (or other warm-season grass) is dormant, many homeowners overseed their lawn in November with a wintergrass (this would be a cool-season grass type such as annual rye). Not only does a wintergrass keep the lawn green all winter, but it crowds out many weeds.

HOW TO APPLY HERBICIDES

Never spray an herbicide on a windy day—it's going to drift. Always wear rubber or disposable plastic gloves, and keep a set of measuring spoons and cups in your garage just for lawn products. Wash them and your sprayer *thoroughly* after using. Then do it again—and again if you plan to use the sprayer for anything other than herbicides.

When I spray a lawn I like to go to the far end of the yard and walk across it in a zig-zag pattern, slightly overlapping the previously sprayed area as I work my way back. This way I don't step in the spray at all.

Liquid Sprays

Most weeds are best attacked during periods of soft, new growth, usually in mid-spring or early fall. Herbicides can be applied in liquid (spray) or granular form. You'll get faster results with a liquid if you apply it correctly. The key to making your liquid spray herbicide work is getting it to stick to the plants. One reason your spray might not stick is that the grass is wet, so **always spray herbicides on a dry lawn.** A second reason is that certain weeds and grasses, especially under hot and dry conditions, produce a protective film that is meant to prevent loss of water. This film also sheds water. There are methods of handling this problem. One is to add a "sticker" to your herbicide, to help the spray stick to a plant. Better garden centers sell stickers. Safer Insecticidal Soap is a natural sticker that can be used with many products.

Another way of getting the spray to stick to the plant is to administer a soap and water treatment. The soap cleans off dirt and breaks down the protective film on the plant. When the soap and water dries you can apply the herbicide.

Tank Sprayers

As I mentioned earlier, I don't trust the hose-end sprayers when exact proportions are critical. With a tank sprayer you can mix the exact amount of herbicide with water, shake it up, and know precisely what is coming out of your sprayer. You can also hold the spraying nozzle close to the ground to avoid drifting.

Spot-Spraying

You can buy premixed herbicides in spray bottles, or to save money you can make up your own mix and put it in your own bottle. **Be sure to mark the bottle clearly and store it as you would any poison.** Spot-spraying is best when you have only scattered weeds here and there. Why waste time and money treating your whole yard, when spot-spraying is all you need? If you are spraying a non-selective herbicide, keep the spray bottle close to the weed and/or use a shield of some type (plastic and cardboard both work well) to prevent damage to surrounding grass.

Granular Herbicides

Some people find it more convenient to spread weedkillers with their fertilizer spreader. There is no mixing involved this way, and less cleaning up afterward. The better granular formulations are ground up into small particles that cover well. For greatest accuracy, use a drop spreader, slightly overlapping the swaths you make.

The visible particles make it easy to ensure full coverage. Never fill the spreader on the lawn. Spillage is hard to avoid and concentrated spills are toxic.

Unlike the liquid sprays, granular weed killers stick best when the weeds are wet. They are therefore best applied after a rain, in the early morning when the dew is thick, or after you've sprinkled the lawn.

A preliminary soap and water washing would be extremely beneficial. In fact, you can use the same soap and water to clean out the spreader when you're finished.

Both liquid and granular weed killers work best if they are given twenty-four hours to work before being washed off, though liquids usually are effective after 4–8 hours of contact. So check the weather before applying.

WHEN TO CALL IN THE PROFESSIONALS

If you have a highly weed-infested lawn, it is definitely worth your while to hire the services of a spray company. See if you can have your lawn treated for weeds without it being fertilized chemically at the same time. Professionals really can do a better job than most homeowners would. If your lawn is treated in the early spring or early fall, you'll still have time to reseed after the weeds have shriveled away. Midsummer treatments are not recommended; wait until early fall for better results.

If you do your own weed killing, use common sense and keep your chemicals away from anything else that could be damaged. Some weedkillers kill shrubs or young trees if spread in their root zone. The package will caution you about this and other hazards. **Please read and follow the directions.**

You might think it strange that I devote so much time to chemical weed control. After all, this book is about getting away from chemicals, isn't it? Exactly. Until you get your weeds under control, I know that many of you will still feel the need to use chemicals. So I want you to learn as much as you can about how to apply them, or how they should be applied by someone else. Make chemicals work with one correct application instead of many haphazard applications. If you follow most of the other principles in this book at the same time, you'll simply out-create the weeds and end up with a thick, reasonably weed-free lawn.

14♦MOWING, SPRAYING, AND FERTILIZING SERVICES

MOWING SERVICES

It seems that every year more people are hiring companies to mow their lawns. Perhaps this is because homeowners are too busy, or maybe because they are more affluent than in years past. Some have told me they use a service because there aren't any neighborhood kids cutting lawns anymore, or that if they do cut lawns, they cut poorly or don't show up regularly. You'll find lists of dozens of mowing companies in any city or suburban phone directory. Still more companies advertise in neighborhood newspapers or on bulletin boards at the local supermarket. Anyone with a lawn mower can start a lawn cutting service. But just because they cut lawns doesn't mean they know how to cut lawns.

Companies vary in numerous and important ways. Some consist solely of one man—the owner—cutting lawns himself. Some include a helper or two, while others operate with one or more foremen and their crews. Ask how often they will cut: whenever the lawn needs cutting? Once a week? How many other customers' lawns will be cut by the same crew each week? What happens if the weather is bad? Do they bill by the cut, the month, the hour, or by some other formula? Will they remove leaves from the lawn in the fall, or just stop mowing? What do they do about grass clippings—leave them on the lawn? Bag them up? Haul them away? Will they edge your walks? Do they adjust cutting heights to individual lawns, or is it a one-height-cuts-all operation? Do they use large mowers (too large), weed whackers, and air blowers (to do a tidy job)? Are they licensed, insured, and charging sales tax on their work? If they don't charge sales tax (in those states that collect it) then they are *probably* not covering their employees with workman's compensation or disability insurance. They might not be licensed or insured, either. How much do the crew members really know about lawn care? Few companies will answer these questions in a similar way; their answers will help you make your choice.

Most services try to cut your lawn once a week. Ideally, they should cut only when necessary, skipping a cut whenever the lawn doesn't need it. And you should have to pay only for each cut. My experience has shown me that the major objective of lawn crews is to finish cutting all the lawns on their route by the end of the week. Time and weather make this a challenge. If you are paying by the cut, they will certainly be more inclined to cut your lawn when they ought to skip it. If you pay by the month, they'll be more inclined to skip a cut when they should cut it. What you might try to work out is that you'll pay by the month, but if they skip a cut, they'll do some trimming or edging instead. The companies can more than make up any missed mowing time by removing leaves on the lawn in the fall.

Whichever way you work it out, try to stay in communication with the crew. Let the workers know if you want the lawn higher, or if you want them to skip cuts during midsummer droughts. Do your part with watering and fertilizing and they will have a nicer lawn to take pride in. If you find out that they don't know much about lawns, try to educate them with this book.

Lawn mowing during hot weather is tough work that doesn't pay much. Dehydration, dizziness, and sun stroke are common. An offer of a cold drink is more welcome than you could imagine. And because you have shown concern for the crew, when you suggest that they sharpen their blades or raise the cutting height, they'll be much more inclined to please you.

FERTILIZING SERVICES

Under the best of conditions your lawn will have no major problems, but suppose you want someone other than yourself to fertilize it and keep an eye out for trouble? You might be able to find a local company that advertises natural or organic fertilizers. I found one near me that manufactures its own blended natural fertilizer and follows the basic principles of this book. They (Chem-Free) have many natural solutions available, but will apply chemicals as a last resort. Call around and you might find a company or landscaper with a private stock of natural fertilizers. If there are no companies in your area with these types of fertilizers, your next best bet (aside from getting some natural fertilizers and applying them yourself) would be to find a company that applies a slow-release, granular fertilizer. There should be no trouble finding such a service.

SPRAYING SERVICES

Let's say you need a spraying company because your lawn is half weeds. Don't believe for a second that any weedkiller is totally safe—who knows what we'll find out thirty years down the road. If you have decided on a chemical weedkiller, make sure it is applied right the first time. Look for the company that has what seems to you the most reasonable approach toward weed control. Get its guarantee. Find out what type of equipment it uses. The large tanks that spray liquid herbicides are more effective than the spreaders that apply the granular types. The granular types only stick to the weeds if they are wet, while the liquid types can be applied when the lawn is dry. Some companies add a substance to make the spray more sticky so it can be applied to a wet lawn as well. It is usually possible to hire a company for only one or two weed sprayings. By thickening up your lawn and keeping it high, you'll discourage most future weeds from getting a foothold.

If you have an insect-infested lawn that you've determined must be handled quickly by chemicals, don't choose just anybody who offers to spray for you. The key to effective insect control will probably be the staying power of the chemical applied, which means that the chemicals must be selected judiciously. Some insects can be controlled by one application of the correct insecticide. Other insects, however, lay eggs that hatch after the adults have been exterminated. Will the insecticide still be there waiting for the eggs a few months down the line? And how dangerous is this chemical to other life? Get information from a few companies and make an educated choice. Once you've identified the insect, check the garden centers and catalogs to see if there is a natural solution to try first.

Lawn treatment professionals have become for many people a necessary part in the maintenance of lawn health. It is clear to me that these professionals mostly treat symptoms, and often unwittingly cause new problems. But times are slowly changing, and the creation of health in order to prevent diseases is becoming a more acceptable idea. Integrated Pest Management programs attempt to reduce excessive chemical spraying by combining many natural methods. This approach is gaining acceptance from many chemical spray companies. Whenever all-natural methods are just as profitable and workable as their chemical counterparts, there is little argument about switching over. Thousands of people rely on lawn chemicals to earn their living. As with any other business, what really counts is results . . . and the bottom line.

GUIDELINES FOR THE FUTURE

With each new year I expect more alternatives to straight chemical lawn treatment to be available. The lawn spraying companies have a responsibility to keep themselves informed and educated so they can provide the best and safest service. Here are some of the specific changes I would like to see:

1. Require professional applicators of lawn chemicals to be certified to handle equipment and chemicals, as well as fully educated about how lawns grow. Part of that knowledge would include natural lawn care theories and practices.

2. Lawn care companies should educate homeowners about lawn care with more than a slip of paper saying to cut higher or give more water.

3. Each company should develop a natural fertilizing program and offer it as an alternative. I know of natural fertilizer manufacturers that would be very willing to supply fertilizers to lawn care companies.

4. Companies should only apply what is needed. Why douse a whole lawn with weedkiller when there are only a few weeds? More *spot treatment* of problems needs to happen.

5. More research and development of natural weed, insect, and disease controls, and at the same time development of replacements for the unsafe chemicals currently being used. Lawns are not food crops; the nation won't die if there are a few weeds or insects in the neighborhood. Applicating companies should ask themselves whether it is worth the risk to use any chemical of questionable safety.

6. Each applicator should be required by the industry to wear gloves, mask, and protective clothing. Many don't. Last year I shook hands with a chemical applicator, and later made the mistake of resting my chin on my hand at my desk. My face itched all day with a mild rash. I don't believe any of the lawn chemicals should be allowed on or into a person's body. Of course, a few years from now research-ers will probably prove scientifically how hazardous these chemicals really are. Why take chances?

7. Mandatory posting of warning signs on lawns that have been sprayed. Some states already have this law. The homeowner who does his own chemical lawn treatment should also have to post warning signs. In fact, his chances of overapplication are greater than the trained pro's.

8. More work on the development of driftless chemicals and drift-free methods of application. Considering the fact that sometimes it's impossible to give advance notice of a spraying, there should be products that aren't going to drift into people's homes and lungs.

The lawn chemical industry has done an amazing job of beautifying the lawns of North America and other parts of the world. But we've come to the point at which scientific research must turn its attention to safety. Prevention and real cures are slowly replacing the treat-the-symptoms way of thinking. You can see evidence of this change everywhere. It can also apply to your lawn.

15 ♦ GROUND COVERS AND MULCHES

Sometimes it is just about impossible to coax a lawn to grow. Perhaps the growing area is too dry, too wet, or too shady. The best shade grasses you can find won't survive under the old tree, and the tree's roots stick up into the lawn to make your job even more difficult. Bare soil is an eyesore on your property, and kids constantly track it into the house. If you can't easily change the conditions that are preventing grass from growing, or if you don't want grass at all, a simple solution is a ground cover, a mulch, or both.

WHAT IS A GROUND COVER?

A ground cover is a bed of low-growing, spreading, or multiplying plants. These plants fill in areas rapidly and will grow under conditions that make decent lawns impossible. They also require very little maintenance. Ground covers are not used solely for difficult lawn areas. They are often included in landscape designs as part of bed or foundation plantings. Oftentimes they provide erosion protection. A full discussion of their uses would take up an entire book. For now, we will view them as alternatives to grass.

Ground covers in lawns are most often used to fill in shady or difficult-to-mow areas. Here is a list of some of the more popular ground cover plants and their attributes.

Bugleweed (*Ajuga*). Ajuga is found in all but the hottest climates. It is a 6-inch plant which spreads quickly by its roots and produces dark blue flowers. It tolerates both sunny and shady conditions.

Candytuft (*Iberis sempervirens*). This eight-inch evergreen is popular because of its clusters of white flowers in May and June. It spreads slowly by aboveground runners, grows in the sun or shade, and will grow in most of the United States.

Candytuft.

Bugleweed.

Common violet.

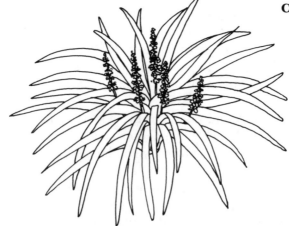

Creeping lilyturf.

English ivy.

Lily-of-the-valley.

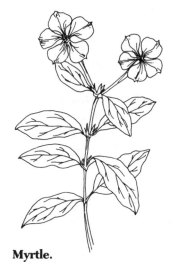

Myrtle.

Pachysandra.

Sedum.

Common violet (*Viola sororial*). This 5–8-inch plant grows in sun or shade and can be a nuisance in a lawn. It makes an excellent ground cover—spreads rather fast by dropping seeds, and produces pretty flowers. Quite hardy.

Creeping lilyturf (*Liriope spicata*). This beautiful evergreen grows in the mid-Atlantic and southern climates. It has lavender, bell-shaped flowers on spikes up to fifteen inches tall. Liriope tolerates sun or shade, heat, salt, drought, and poor soil. Some people actually use it as a grass because it has similar foliage.

English ivy (*Hedera helix*) or **baltic ivy** (*Hedera helix* cv. 'Baltica'). A creeping ground cover that can also be a climbing vine, English ivy forms a thick (9-inch), fast-spreading evergreen mat that turns slightly purple in the winter. Ivy roots quickly as it spreads, so it is very useful on slopes.

Lily-of-the-valley (*Convallaria majalis*). You need a well-drained soil for this very fast-spreading, six-inch-tall plant. It spreads by underground stems and dies back each fall. Each May or June it produces wonderfully scented white, bell-shaped flowers. It grows in sun or shade.

Myrtle or **periwinkle** (*Vinca minor*). This is a 4–9 inch evergreen with oval leaves along a wiry stem. Its light, violet-blue flowers bloom in late spring and early summer. *V. minor* spreads both by roots and aboveground runners. It will prevent erosion once established, and it can grow in sun or shade in a slightly moist soil. It will survive as far south as the Gulf Coast.

Pachysandra (*P. terminalis*, Japanese spurge). An eight-inch evergreen with dark, glossy leaves, pachysandra will grow in shade or sun in all but the extremely hot or cold sections of North America. It prefers a moist, loose soil and spreads slowly with underground roots and stems to form new plants. Occasional cutting back will accelerate spreading. The white flower spikes are barely noticeable.

Sedum (stonecrop, live-forever). There are many varieties of sedum, noted for their fleshy, swollen leaves indicative of many plants that have to survive in sunny, dry conditions. They take the full sun. Some varieties have colorful flowers, and a few are evergreens.

Any plant that tends to spread and isn't too high can be used as a ground cover. You can be very imaginative with your choice as long as it will grow under its planting conditions. Lilies, ferns, herbs, flowers, vines, bulbs, and even special grasses can function as ground covers. Small shrubs such as low-growing junipers or euonymus will spread over a slope or bed with or without rerooting along the way, and can still function as ground covers. Check with your nursery keeper to see what he or she would suggest. You'll get a broad view that won't limit you to the common ground covers.

PLANTING PROCEDURES

If you want ground cover you'll have to get rid of whatever grass you have in the planting area. This shouldn't be too difficult—sometimes a quick scraping with a hoe is all you need. Other times the grass must be dug out, tilled under, or covered over.

To encourage a ground cover to grow well, you'll need to prepare a bed 6–8 inches deep. If you're competing with tree roots, add soil and organic matter to build up a bed. In other situations you can turn over or till up the soil. Whenever you are making a new bed, mix in at least two inches of organic matter. Use aged leaves, clippings, sawdust, compost, manures, and peat moss. If some of the materials aren't aged enough (not even partially decomposed), add a high nitrogen fertilizer to speed up decomposition. Let it work a couple of weeks before planting.

Most ground covers need a good soil to help compensate for the poor conditions that caused you to plant them to begin with. The better soil will help the ground cover establish itself quickly, and will facilitate spreading and multiplying. You should build up a bed higher than the lawn so it will drain easily, and for aesthetic purposes as well. The general rule: the smaller the plant, the closer the spacing in the bed. Keep the plants from drying out. A 1–2-inch layer of shredded wood mulch will conserve moisture and discourage weed growth.

Take good care of the young plants, and before you know it they'll be established and spreading on their own. Check with your nursery keeper for the specific requirements of the plants you buy.

You'll find that whether you plant a patch of ground cover under

AREAS COVERED BY 100 PLANTS AT A GIVEN SPACING*

Planting Distance in Inches	Square Feet Covered by 100 Plants
4	11
6	25
8	44
10	70
12	100
15	156
18	225
24	400
36	900
48	1600

• Spacing calculated from the center of one plant to the center of the next plant.

trees, on a steep incline, or in another difficult-to-mow area, it will look great and be almost maintenance-free. Scout around the affluent sections of town and you'll find ground covers used freely and wisely. Just remember, ground cover plants are not as durable as a thick lawn. They should not be walked on much, if at all. If you need a path through a section of ground cover, install stepping stones or something smaller. If the area is going to get a lot of traffic—enough to ruin a ground cover—try a mulch instead.

MULCHES

The term **mulch** covers a broad spectrum of soil-covering materials, from wood chips to rocks to plastic. Most of the commonly used mulching materials function much like the naturally deposited mulches they are meant to imitate.

To get a clear concept of what a mulch really is, think about the soil surface in the woods. It is covered by a layer of leaves or needles dropped from the trees. This layer doesn't get very thick because it is continuously decomposing and returning to the soil. It keeps out competitive weeds, protects the soil from drying, prevents erosion by letting rains seep in, maintains a steady soil temperature, and enriches the soil as it decomposes. This is a real mulch.

Humans have taken a cue from nature and utilize mulching in home landscapes, gardens, and farms. Unfortunately, most homeowners use mulching material more for beauty and weed prevention than for soil enrichment. Rocks, gravel, plastic, and large chunks of bark do not readily decompose, though they do make an effective covering for otherwise bare or weedy soil.

Landscape Fabric

A common practice today is to install a "permanent" landscape fabric which isn't meant to decompose. This fabric is a woven plastic that allows air and water to pass, but won't let weeds grow through. Mulch is spread on top of it, and never comes in contact with the soil. This method allows you to put down bark chips that won't sink into the soil. I would never install a stone or gravel mulch without landscape fabric underneath to choke out weeds. Hand weeding a bed of gravel is almost impossible.

Whenever you use landscape fabric you prevent the growth of new plants, ground covers included. But one can always cut holes in the fabric and plant individual flowers or shrubs. Spread on a thick layer of mulch, thick enough to prevent light from reaching the fabric, and border your mulch with timber, a trench, plastic edging, bricks, or whatever you please to keep the mulch contained.

Natural Mulches

If you want a mulch that will decompose into the bed, you need to use real mulches. These are organic materials such as cocoa shells, peat moss, shredded bark, grass clippings, and leaves that won't take years to decompose. There might be others available in your neighborhood. Lay them on a good 2–4 inches thick, expecting to add more each year. The mulch will keep the soil in good shape and will allow ground cover to spread without difficulty. You might get a few weeds in it, but they'll pull out easily. Real mulch attracts beneficial soil organisms and worms, and constantly improves the soil.

Use shredded wood or small (1-inch) gravel on areas that get a lot of foot traffic. For slopes you can use all but the finer mulches (peat moss, cocoa shells). Most will hold without washing away in a rainstorm. For durability and longevity, nothing beats stone products set on landscape fabric. Chunk bark is used mostly for its attractiveness surrounding shrubs and trees.

Why bother trying to get lawn to grow where it doesn't want to? Instead, cover the area with mulch, plant some flowers or ground cover if you like, and add a manicured look to your yard.

16♦LAWN CALENDAR

Now that we've reached the end of the book, it is safe to write out a month-by-month guideline for lawn care. Had I put this in the beginning, many readers would not have bothered to learn all the basics. Knowledge of these principles allows you to think for yourself and act responsibly. It gives you the ability to formulate your decisions according to your own lawn's particular conditions. There is nothing so important to natural lawn care as this.

Natural lawn care means a desire to work with the underlying causes of both lawn sickness and lawn health. It means treating the true causes rather than the symptoms of poor lawn health—even if you must treat these symptoms initially. The goal is to create a healthy lawn by building a healthy soil. As I said in the introduction, the idea of creating health to prevent illness is not new, it's just new to lawn care. Try it for yourself. I think you will be happy with the results, and proud of yourself for achieving them naturally.

MARCH Spring clean-up. Rake your lawn with a bamboo or spring-steel rake. Remove all debris and try to lift (gently) any matted grass. Spread snow piles around so they melt faster. Inspect carefully for bare and thin areas, and for the peeling turf that indicates grub damage. Sections with snow mold, mosses, and disease should be raked and treated with natural controls. Lime can be applied at this time. In the South, seeding, sprigging, and plug-planting can be done as soon as the ground is workable. If you had a wintergrass growing, cut it short to open it up for the warm-season grass. Don't walk on soggy lawns.

APRIL Work to repair any damage you spotted during spring clean-up. Spot-seed and fertilize sections that look bad. Apply natural insect controls if they're needed. Roll only the sandiest of soils to level a lawn out. Clay soils will compact with rolling, so fill in dips with half-inch topdressings of light soil every two weeks. Cut the lawn low

151

at first and gradually raise the height. Keep mower blades sharp. If crabgrass was a problem last year, rake it out of the lawn, reseed, fertilize, and then apply a safe-for-grass-seed pre-emergent (if desired). Dethatching is safe until mid-May. Core aerating is okay until early June. Treat lawns with severe thatch or poor soil with a natural soil conditioner. New lawns can be seeded as soon as the soil is dry and workable. In the South you can sprig-plant, plug-plant, or seed at this time.

MAY Cut the grass high and frequently with sharp blades. Chemically treat broadleaf weeds now, if you must. A crabgrass pre-emergent can still be applied. Hold off watering in the North. Make sure the grass is growing tall before the weather turns hot. In the South this is the best time to put in a new lawn. Late May is right for the principal fertilization of the year (or break it up into lighter April and June fertilizings).

JUNE Cool-season grasses should be fertilized in late May or early June, before it gets hot. Keep lawns high to crowd out crabgrass. Treat with natural soil conditioner if it's called for. Watch for insects. Spot-kill weeds. Water only if necessary, since high humidity encourages disease. In the South there is still time for a new lawn, but the soil must be kept moist for the young plants—wait until the end of summer, if possible. Watch for insects.

JULY Mow lawns high! In the North water every week-to-ten-days if you want to prevent dormancy. Hand pull smaller numbers of weeds. In the South water once a week to keep the lawn healthy while it is vigorously growing. Use soap and water treatments on insects and disease.

AUGUST In the North watch for insects—especially sod webworm. Don't cut a dormant lawn. If the lawn is growing, keep your mower blades very sharp and never cut too much at once. Mid-August is the ideal time to prepare the ground for seeding. Keep it moist and remove sprouting weeds until early September. Keep southern lawns high, and water them weekly. This is the time of year for light fertilizing. A pre-emergent for annual bluegrass can be applied, if necessary.

SEPTEMBER This is the best time for repairing northern lawns. Finish seeding by mid-September. Dethatching and aerating should be completed before mid-October; fertilize immediately afterward. Apply natural soil conditioner to lawns with severe thatch or poor soil. Remove weeds that sprouted over the summer. In colder sections give the lawn its main fertilizing for the year (2 pounds nitrogen in a balanced natural fertilizer per 1000 square feet).

Dethatch and aerate southern lawns in September and October. Keep the grass high if you don't plan to overseed a wintergrass. Otherwise, begin to mow your lawn shorter. Fertilize now if you intend to plant a wintergrass.

OCTOBER Northern lawns in milder areas should receive their principal fertilization now. Prevent leaves from matting on the lawn. Don't neglect the grass at this time—it needs to be green and fairly long. Gradually bring the height down to about 1½ inches. Stay off the lawn when it's wet until it stops growing.

Allow southern lawns to go dormant, or, if you are going to plant a wintergrass, cut them short. Remove thatch and debris and overseed with cool-season grass (perennial or annual ryegrass or bluegrass) toward the end of the month. The ideal time for this would be after dethatching. Topdress lawns with a light soil and then roll with a near-empty roller to bring seed and soil into contact. Keep the soil moist until the new grass becomes established.

NOVEMBER In the North, keep leaves off the grass. Apply lime if you need to. Empty the gas from your mower and perform end-of-season maintenance. In the South, handle any weeds that pop up on dormant lawns. Perform mower maintenance. Plant wintergrass during this month. Keep the lawn cut at 2½–3 inches until the weather turns hot and your warm-season grass is ready to take over.

DECEMBER-JANUARY In the South, wherever there is no wintergrass, hand pull weeds in your spare time.

FEBRUARY Read your catalogs; order some natural products for the new season.

17 ◆ PARTING WORDS

Building a healthy lawn naturally is a positive, constructive approach to lawn care. Your main concern is to create a rich, porous topsoil, and a thick, deep-rooted, thatch-free lawn that will flourish and keep the pests at bay. This book has tried to give you a clear picture of what a healthy lawn and soil should be like. Now that you know, set your sights on achieving these goals.

A DOZEN WAYS TO A HEALTHY LAWN

1. Keep the lawn clean and standing straight. Your spring clean-up should remove any debris and lift matted grass.

2. Fill in bare spots with new grass before weeds fill them in. If grassy weeds (such as crabgrass) are a problem, a pre-emergent applied correctly will prevent their sprouting and allow you to fill in with good grass.

3. Treat weak-looking or diseased spots with an early fertilizing. I use a high microorganism fertilizer such as Lawn Restore, Lawns Alive, Fertrel, Erth-Rite, seaweed, or similar products.

4. Have a soil test done. You will find out your soil pH—an overly acid or alkaline soil will make nutrients unavailable; test for nutrient content in the soil; get a strong idea of what your soil needs.

5. Remove thatch. It will encourage almost every lawn problem that you could possibly have. Do this in the spring or early fall.

6. Aerate the lawn and soil. Aeration breaks through thatch and opens up the soil to help reduce compaction. It encourages deeper rooting and makes watering easier on heavy or hard-to-wet soils. Aerate once a year on a good lawn, twice a year (spring and fall) on a poor lawn. Fertilize right afterward.

7. Fertilize naturally. Build a healthy soil environment by adding fertilizers that are alive with beneficial microorganisms. They'll bring out the best in your soil and will help create better soil structure from within. They also help speed up decomposition of clippings and thatch. The slow release of the nutrients keeps grass from growing too fast. Add ground limestone if needed when you fertilize (as long as you aren't seeding at the same time).

8. Mow the right way. Don't cut the lawn too short. Keep the blade sharp and never cut off too much at once. Look at the grass in front of you, and not the calendar. Cut when needed. High grass will crowd out crabgrass.

9. Water deeply. Light watering keeps the roots at the surface and makes for weaker grass and thatch formation. Water every 7-10 days (only if needed) on heavier soils—slightly more on light, sandy soils.

10. Keep pests at bay naturally. Sometimes a little soap and water is all you need. There are natural products available now to cover almost every lawn problem. Thatch is pests' favorite environment.

11. Control weeds. Taller, thicker lawns crowd out many weed types. Controlling soil compaction and too wet or dry soils will eliminate others. Dig out or spot-spray individual weeds. If you must use an herbicide on the whole lawn to treat a bad situation, do it correctly so you won't have to do it again. Then work at building up the lawn and soil.

12. Keep it green in the fall. Don't neglect the lawn or start cutting too short. You can lower the height of the lawn when growth slows down, but keep it green. Green blades mean food production (for winter storage) and root growth. September is the best month for lawn repair, thatch removal, seeding, aerating, and fertilizing. Keep leaves from matting on the grass and don't let any leaves stay on the grass over the winter.

IS ANYBODY LISTENING?

The answer to that question is a definite yes! The lawn care industry is changing rapidly, fueled by public demand for safer products. Check the shelves of any garden center and you will see how things are changing.

Most professional applicators now offer a no-pesticide, or reduced-pesticide program. Some offer natural fertilizers. And most will apply some form of synthetic-organic fertilizer. Horticultural oils and soaps are replacing or reducing insecticide applications. Professionals are trying to educate customers about higher mowing practices and are encouraging them to water deeply and leave clippings on the lawn.

Even local governments are getting into the act. Some communities, finding that 20–30 percent of their landfills are made up of yard waste, are *requiring* homeowners to leave clippings on the lawn. Some are composting clippings and leaves and selling or giving it back to the homeowners.

This is all great news. The professionals and community leaders are listening. They are responding to the public's desires. And, better yet, they are taking the initiative to develop safer solutions on their own. Changes in lawn care are going to play an important role in this "Decade of the Environment." This book should make it a little easier for you to learn how to do your part.

Appendix: Resources

Who to Write To

Bio-Integral Resource Center
P.O. Box 7414
Berkeley, CA 94707

Biological Urban Gardening Services (BUGS)
P.O. Box 76
Citrus Heights, CA 95611

The Lawn Institute
1509 Johnson Ferry Rd., NE
Suite 190
Marietta, GA 30062

National Coalition Against the Misuse of Pesticides
530 7th St. S.E.
Washington, D.C. 20003

Rodale Press (*Organic Gardening* magazine)
33 E. Minor St.
Emmaus, PA 18049

Sources of Natural Lawn Care Products

AgriVentures (*grass mats*)
P.O. Box 178A
Briarcliff, NY 10510
914-762-5724

BIO Logic (*Scanmask and biological insect control*)
418 Briar Ln.
Chambersburg, PA 17201
717-263-2789

BIOSYS (*biological insect controls*)
1057 East Meadow Circle
Palo Alto, CA 94303

California Spray Dry Co. (*natural fertilizers*)
P.O. Box 5035
4221 E. Mariposa Rd.
Stockton, CA 95215-0035
209-948-0209

Canton Mills, Inc. (*natural fertilizers and amendments*)
Minnesota City, MN 55959
1-800-328-5349
in Minn. 1-800-247-0309

EarthGro Inc.
Route 207
Lebanon, CT 06249
800-736-7645

Fairfax Biological Lab, Inc.
(*milky spore powder*)
Clinton Corners, NY 12514
914-266-3705

The Fertrell Co. (*fertilizers and
soil amendments*)
P.O. Box 265
Bainbridge, PA 17502
717-367-1566

Four Star Agricultural Services
(*soil conditioners*)
2275 N. State Rd. #1
P.O. Box 463
Bluffton, IN 46714
800-348-2608

Green Earth Organics (*complete
line of natural lawn care
products*)
12310 Hwy. 99 S., Unit 119
Everett, WA 98204
206-845-2321

Green Pro Services (*complete line
of natural products*)
380 S. Franklin St.
Hempstead, NY 11550
800-645-6464
NYS 516-538-6444

Growing Naturally (*complete line
of natural products*)
P.O. Box 54
149 Pine Ln.
Pineville, PA 18946
215-598-7025

Harmony Farm Supply (*complete
range of natural products*)
P.O. Box 451
Graton, CA 95444
707-823-9125

Interstate Brokers, Inc. (*biostimulants, fertilizers*)
Box 254
Westhampton, NY 11977
516-288-1598

Inversand Co. (*Glauconite
[greensand] natural soil conditioner and potash source*)
P.O. Box 45
Clayton, NJ 08312
609-881-2345

Maxicrop U.S.A., Inc. (*natural
fertilizers, sea products*)
P.O. Box 964
Arlington Heights, Il 60006

Medina Agricultural Products
(*soil activator products*)
P.O. Box 309
Highway 90 West
Hondo, Texas 78861
512-426-3011

Mellinger's (*fertilizers, soil conditioners, soil amendments*)
2310 W. South Range Rd.
Lima, OH 44452-9731
800-321-7444

Milwaukee Metropolitan Sewer-
age District (*Milorganite fertilizer*)
735 North Water St.
Milwaukee, WI 53202

Gardens Alive!
5100 Schenley Place
Lawrenceburg, IN 47025
812-537-8650

Necessary Trading Company (*complete line of natural products*)
691 Salem Ave.
New Castle, VA 24127
703-864-5103

Nitron Industries (*complete line of natural products, soil conditioners*)
P.O. Box 1447
Fayetteville, AR 72702
800-835-0123

North Country Organics (*natural fertilizers and soil amendments*)
RR1 Box 2232
Bradford, VT 05033-9729
802-222-4277

Ohio Earth Food, Inc. (*sea products and complete line of natural products*)
13737 DuQuette Ave., N.E.
Hartville, OH 44632
216-877-9356

Organic Lawn Care (*natural fertilizers and soil amendments*)
435 Wilson St. N.E.
Minneapolis, MN 55413
800-798-1069

Plant Right
P.O. Box 282
10125 Christian Rd.
Versailles, OH 45380-0282
800-752-6802

Reuter Labs, Inc. (*natural pest controls*)
8450 Natural Way
Manassas Park, VA 22111

Ringer Research (*complete line of natural products, Lawn Restore fertilizer*)
9959 Valley View Rd.
Eden Prairie, MN 53344-3585
800-654-1047

Safer, Inc. (*pest controls, natural soaps, natural herbicide*)
189 Wells Ave.
Newton, MA 02159
617-964-2990

Soilizer Corporation (*root stimulants*)
25 Science Park
New Haven, CT 05611
203-786-5295

Sustane Corp.
1107 Hazeltine Blvd.
Chaska, MN 55318
612-448-8828

Universal Diatoms (*diatomaceous earth*)
410 12th St. N.W.
Albuquerque, NM 87102
505-247-3271

Zook & Ranck, Inc. (*Erth-Rite fertilizer, soil amendments*)
RD 1 Box 243
Gap, PA 17527

Glossary

Acid soil. Soil with a pH factor below 7.

Aerating (aerifying), mechanical. The process of opening up a compacted soil and/or thatch-ridden lawn by mechanically poking holes, slicing, removing cores, etc. without major damage to the lawn itself.

Aerating, natural. The loosening of compacted soil life. Organisms such as worms, insects, and microbes during the course of their normal activities will help form and maintain a good soil structure. Many of the natural fertilizers contain microbes that speed up the natural aerating process. (*See* **soil conditioners.**)

Alkaline soil. Soil with a pH factor above 7.

Annual, summer. A plant that grows from seed for one season and then dies.

Annual, winter. A plant that grows from seed in the fall, survives the winter, goes to seed the next spring, and then dies.

Blade Brake Clutch (BBC). A mechanism that engages and disengages a lawnmower's blade or blades. This safety feature stops the blade from spinning when you let go of or step away from the mower.

Blend. A combination of two or more varieties (cultivars) of a grass species. Example: Adelphi, Merit, and Fylking—all Kentucky bluegrasses—could be planted together as a blend.

Bunch grass. A grass type that spreads by growing tillers (new stems and leaves) at the base of the mother plant. A bunch grass will normally not send out stolons or rhizomes.

Castings. Digested soil and plant remains that are excreted by earthworms. Castings have a high fertilizer and soil conditioner value.

Colonize. To form patches of similar grass types in a lawn.

Cool-season grasses (Northern grasses). These are grasses that grow best in temperatures of 60 to 75 degrees. They are able to withstand freezing winter temperature, but tend to go dormant during the midsummer heat.

Coring. A method of mechanical aeration by which hollow tines or spoons lift out cores of soil from the ground at 4- to 6-inch intervals.

Crown. The main growth center for the aboveground parts of the grass plant. It is located at or near the soil surface at the base of the stems.

Cultivar. A specific variety of a grass species with its own distinguishable characteristics. Example: Koket, Banner, and Jamestown are all cultivars of fine fe. cue.

Dethatch. To remove thatch by mechanical means or hand raking.

Diatomaceous earth. Skeletal remains of a class of algae which are ground into razor-sharp, minute particles and used for insect control. Diatomaceous earth is harmless to earthworms, birds, and mammals yet it will deter grubs, chinch bugs, and many garden pests.

Dormant. Inactive. A temporary cessation of the aboveground growth of a plant due to extreme heat, cold, or drought.

Enzymes. Complex proteins or organic substances that serve to initiate or accelerate chemical reactions and exchanges. Enzymes can release otherwise locked-up soil and plant nutrients; they speed up microbial activity and help to open up the soil for air, water, and root penetration.

Endophytes. Fungi that grow within the tissues of certain grasses producing no external sign of infection. Although some strains of endophytes are toxic in forage grasses (used for grazing animals), they can be quite beneficial in turf grasses. Some of the benefits are insect resistance, increased tillering, better ability to withstand heat, draught, and injury, and more aggressive growth in general (which would aid in weed control).

Fertilizer burn. Dehydration injury to grass caused by high concentration of chemicals (salts) sucking water out of the grass plant.

Germinate. To sprout. Seeds are dormant until they germinate.

Germination rate. The percentage of a quantity of seed which will germinate under normal conditions. This percentage decreases as the seed ages.

Herbicide. A substance used to kill weeds or unwanted plant growth.

Humus. Organic matter in an advanced stage of decay, the original material having become unrecognizable. Humus is rich in nutrients and full of life. It helps to form topsoil from subsoil, holds water, and promotes good soil structure. It is the ideal soil conditioner.

Larva. The wingless, newly hatched form certain insects assume before they undergo metamorphosis and become adults. Grubs are the larvae of beetles.

Leaf. Consists of two parts in a grass plant. The sheath, found at the base of the leaf, is wrapped around the stem. The blade is the flat part of the leaf that extends outward and upward from the sheath.

Microbe. Short for microorganism. A minute living organism such as bacteria, fungi, algae, protozoa, or yeast.

Mixture. Two or more different grass species planted together. Bluegrass and fescue planted together comprise a mixture.

Mulch. Any material that can be used to cover the soil surface for the purpose of aesthetics, protection and buffering from the elements, walkways, keeping weeds down, and preventing erosion—to name a few. Mulches made from shredded or chopped organic matter will enrich the soil as they decompose.

Mulching mower. A mower that chops grass clippings very finely and throws them back onto the lawn, where they will recycle themselves.

Nurse grass (companion grass). A mix of grass seed that is meant to grow fast and provide temporary cover and soil stabilization while the more desirable grasses grow in. Nurse grasses are usually annual grasses or types that easily get choked out by the desirable grass.

Organic matter. Any material that is derived from plant or animal waste.

Overseed. To spread seed over an existing lawn, either to help thicken it or to introduce a new grass type. (*See* **winter seeding.**)

pH. A numerical measure of alkalinity or acidity. Below 7 is acid, above 7 is alkaline. Seven is neutral.

Photosynthesis. The process by which a plant (in its chlorophyll-containing cells) makes carbohydrates (food) from sunlight, carbon dioxide, and water.

Plug. A small piece of sod that can be used to introduce a new grass type into a lawn, or to start a new lawn on a prepared bed. Plugs (or biscuits) are normally spaced at intervals of ten inches or more.

Rhizome. An underground shoot or stem that will root and form a new plant at a distance from the mother plant.

Scalp. To cut the lawn too short, removing most of the green growth and exposing crowns and the base of the plants.

Sheath. *See* **Leaf.**

Sod. Strips or sections of turfgrass cut away from the ground in which it is growing along with roots and adhering soil.

Soil conditioner. Any product that improves the physical properties of the soil. Conditioners open up a compacted soil by causing particles to form granules or crumbs with space between them. They help bond sandy soils in the same manner. Some conditioners also contain enzymes, humus, or other microbes that help maintain and improve soil properties.

Soil probe (sampling tube). A hollow tube that can be inserted into the soil to remove a section of it. One side of the tube is cut away to provide a view of the soil, roots, thatch, etc.

Sprigs. Stolons or rhizomes (and sometimes tillers) which can be planted at intervals in a prepared bed to form a new lawn.

Stolon. An aboveground shoot or stem that grows along the soil surface. It can root at any of its nodes (joints) and form new plants.

Thatch. A matted layer of grass stems, roots, clippings, stolons, rhizomes, and other plant debris that sits on top of the soil, choking out the grass plant. Thatch also keeps fertilizer and water from reaching the soil, and it provides a home to undesirable insects and diseases. When thatch is very thick, the grass will send its roots into the thatch instead of the soil.

Tiller. A lateral (forming on the side) shoot or stem emanating from the mother plant. Bunch grasses enlarge by growing more and more tillers.

Topdressing. Spreading a layer of soil or a prepared soil mix (not more than a half-inch thick) over a lawn and raking or brooming it over to work it down to the soil surface. Low spots can be raised by topdressing every few weeks.

Turfgrass. Any species of grass that is meant to be maintained as a mowed lawn (as opposed to forage grasses and ornamental grasses).

Vertical mower. A machine with vertical blades every inch or so that slice through the lawn and thatch. It is used for thatch removal, lawn renovation, and opening up the lawn to provide room for seeds to reach the soil when overseeding or winter seeding.

Warm-season grasses (southern grasses). These are grasses that grow best in temperature of 80 to 95 degrees (F). They go dormant (aboveground) in the winter in the South, even if temperatures rarely reach freezing. They cannot survive cold northern winters.

W.I.N. Water-insoluble, slow-release nitrogen. In this form nitrogen releases slowly into the soil rather than as soon as it contacts water. The nitrogen in most natural fertilizers is W.I.N. Synthetic W.I.N. is often combined with quick-release water-soluble nitrogen in chemical fertilizers.

Winter seeding. Practiced on warm-season lawns that turn brown over the winter. A cool-season grass is seeded over the lawn in the fall so there will be green grass throughout the winter. The warm-season grass usually chokes this "wintergrass" out by late spring.

INDEX